The best and most beautiful things in the world cannot be seen or even touched. They must be felt with the heart.

—Helen Keller

LEMURIA REMEMBERED:

Through the Eyes of a Child

By Celeste Eaton

Table of Contents

Dedication

I dedicate this book with deep Love and Gratitude to my special friends who have changed my life through their interactions with me. Thank you Angels, Dolphins, Whales, Big Foot and all my ET friends, seen and unseen. It is through our connection that this book was birthed into being.

Introduction

Please accept this invitation to journey together, joyfully, through two sacred spaces: the liquid blue playground of the dolphins and whales, and the luminous, opalescent realms of angelic beings in Lemuria. The wisdom of these two worlds, populated with ascending beings of love and light, is of immeasurable wealth.

Having graciously spent sacred moments within both worlds, I am now called to share. For in these worlds, swimming with cetacean friends and communicating vibrationally with higher light beings, I have learned much about life and myself from the time of birth to this present moment. It seems I have spent my whole life living and remembering this mystical, magical world by weaving in the mysteries of the unknown and known.

Growing up, I felt like I was living in two different worlds. For most of youth I had a feeling that I didn't belong. It was difficult to understand how or why people around me acted the way they did. School felt like a strange place. I remember in kindergarten I was standing back and watching kids jump rope. I was invited to play, yet was too shy. I felt alone and chose to be alone much of the time, embodying shyness, and only observing others.

When I was nine, we moved inland from Fort Bragg on the California coast to Red Bluff, California, and I realized I had to become like the other kids. I decided not to just observe my classmates, but to participate in their activities. I did this knowing that if I did as they were doing, I would be accepted. I quickly became well liked and began to see myself with more confidence.

In my high school years I stepped a little more out of my shyness, and, to my surprise, I began to receive leadership roles—in the song leader club and the cheerleading squad, and I was even crowned the high school homecoming queen as a senior!

I believe these blessings came to me when I decided to communicate and share my precious memories of the Lemurian Love and Light. By sharing my love and compassion with others from my Higher Lemurian Heart, I was able to honor and value myself. And by embodying more of the frequencies I had hidden away, I began to remember more of the mystical world of Lemuria.

Conveying the highlights of this adventure would be to envision awakening the frequencies of another Timeline. Then, as if "weaving" back and forth through my life one world and another, each co-creating the other, I was evolving into a more true essence of "Who I Am."

The roles I played (and still in play) were all created by myself and the Divine aspects of the Prime Creator, God, Source, All That Is, Higher Self and the Greater Being/Essence. I believe we all have our unique way of communicating the energies that assist each of us in our own lives.

As you probably have sensed, I have led a very unusual life, yet it has been a wonderful life in many ways. My daughters used to say, "Why can't you be a normal mom?" I would reply to them, "I am not a normal mom, I am an angel!" You can imagine what those words meant to them; that says it all!

I can happily say that today my daughters Reneé and Kimberlee are my best friends, I love my family dearly and they love and accept me just the way I am. We have a wonderful relationship in understanding that we are all different, yet alike in so many ways. My family is so very important to me, as I am to them. This is the Lemurian Way.

As a child I communicated with the Fairies and Angels. We spent precious hours together, totally understanding that it was our destiny to come together and learn from each other. I feel I was born into my family and environment to remember and reunite my small self to my larger Self, all the while influenced with memories of living the Lemurian way. These frequencies remained with me as part of "Who I Was Then," from another timeline to the "Who I Am Now," a child of Lemuria Remembering!

Remembering Lemuria wasn't really a remembering from a time past. It has always been within me, from my first embodiment onto Mother Earth at the beginning of the Lemurian cycle. My life mission is to carry the focus and force of the Divine Mother, projecting feminine frequencies to assist others facing challenges, as well as protecting all of our amazing cetaceans, ocean creatures, and our wonderful animal friends on land and air.

All my life I have loved animals and it is my desire to save animals. I have to interrelate the Lemurians' love for animals. From those first moments of remembering to this present moment, this has been my life focus!

There is a lot of information between my entering my first embodiment on the Lemurian timeline to this present timeline. I hope you will enjoy my story. It begins with my connection from living in Mt. Shasta's front yard, literally seeing mystical Mt. Shasta from the picture window of my home. What a blessing.

I would like to convey to each of my readers the true essence and complete fullness of my experiences—the mystical and magical as well as the physical.

I entered the blue water environment of the dolphins and whales in 1994, and for thirty-plus years I have immersed myself in alternative healing modalities of light and sound combined with the teachings of the Cetacean and Celestial Realms, Teachers of Light, as well as many Divine Masters.

Come play and be in joy, as together we share a journey you will never forget!

If paradise is calling you and this sounds like something you'd like to do, then I am here for you! Isn't it time to celebrate your life by living every wondrous moment? I am looking forward to meeting and seeing you here, the reader of these sacred words, as we remember and Birth the New Lemuria of the fifth dimension and beyond!

Chapter 1

Lemuria, The Land Forgotten
Birthing Again on a New Timeline

A Guided Meditation: Journey to Lemuria

When you are ready to journey into the interior of Lemuria, a spark of light will appear in front of you. This spark of glimmering light will begin to grow into human size as a luminescent egg-shaped orb, enfolding you with its shimmering light. You will begin to rise up in your Lemurian bubble of Love and Light. Drifting above all thoughts, feelings and emotions, beyond both logic and reason, moving even beyond time and space, you will find this land that has been forgotten. You will cross the Bridge of Beliefs into the realm of God/Goddess/All That Is and enter upon Lemuria.

As one approaches Lemuria by air, its location is in the Pacific Ocean, far from other landmasses. It appears first with a cloud of mist hanging over a large land mass, Its high Mountain peaks shining like obsidian in the soft mist. One might entirely miss the island when flying over this vista in one's journey beyond beliefs. For one might only see the mist that surrounds it and not the land concealed below.

Yet as you descend and emerge through the mist you see before you a most glorious land, a beautiful, huge island, its waters bluer than any blue you have ever seen, glistening with colors of aquamarine, soft turquoise, steely blue, midnight blue, and the entire spectrum of ocean blue.

This beautiful island, with its white sandy beaches, radiant as crystals of diamonds and silica, has pure energy radiating and emanating in all directions from all objects. All color seems more brilliant, more alive here.

And the ocean, changing green and blue with the passing of the hour, is stunning. Gleaming colors of the brilliant sun shine through the soft mist and mix with the amazing blue of the sky.

To the East and West of the island, beaches yield to lush forests, before giving way to rolling green foothills. The magic and mystic land of Lemuria's Interior is encircled with Mountains that provide protection. The interior is known as the Mystic Land of Lemuria.

Those called to these inner lands were called in their dreams, or from their mystical undertakings, or invited by those of the interior. If you didn't enter, it was not a decision based in fear, but rather out of respect. It was not for you to go there.

To the North and East, timberlands shifted into farmlands and rolling hills. Most of the populations lived in the periphery. Here countryside and families united.

In the South and West, Mountains retired to the sea and were home to rich mining lodes. This protected area was abundant with profitable items used for mystical experience, including many powerful healing Lemurian crystals.

The North to true West was punctuated with jagged cliffs where high flat lands and fields of tall grass thrived until they met the high cliffs and dropped severely.

The North was home to rugged Mountain ranges and rivers that poured straight out to sea. This land was uninhabitable. Inside these Mountains lay the sacred interior.

Lemuria's Interior

Children would be called to go to the interior through their dreams. Knowing they were called to go for this special training, mystics and dreamers would travel here during solstices, equinoxes or special events to seek out travelers, witnesses and dreamers. Honored invitation was given as a message by a Teacher, a Healer, or from Keepers of the Flame of Truth.

These children were called "Crystal Climbers." Mystics would bring them and gather those who would travel to the interior. If you were called in by a dream or by insight during meditation, you would travel for weeks, months, years, or even a decade to get to your destination.

Once inside the interior, pillars and columns of stone rise above the lushness of the tropical forest. Those called (Crystal Climbers) would sit at the base of these pillars and learn to teleport by altering energies, frequencies and their very molecules.

Crystal Climbers would sometimes sit for up to six months before they were ready. When the time was right, they would disappear/teleport 100 to 200 feet up and then reappear or rematerialize.

Here, above the stone pillars, the enormous Golden Light Crystal Cities lived. This was your only way to get to the top of the Crystal Cities. Only those called could be there, so no one could judge anyone. No one was questioned because if you couldn't go, you didn't belong.

This was the first concept of Heaven with its golden crystal lights. It was like Shangri-la, these cities of gold and light, cities of Healing, Teaching and Dreaming. To fulfill your destiny you could spend ten, twenty or thirty years here. When it was time to go, to return to the exterior, it was done as a Witness or a Guardian of the Light.

Having gained the wisdom needed for those who were to dream dreams for others, the Crystal Climbers would once again teleport and materialize in the world. It may not be from where they came, but it would be to where they were called to do what had been learned.

Teachers to teach, Witnesses to witness, Guardians to guard the light and the Flame of Truth, and the Dreamers would go forth and dream the dream.

Lemurian Dreamers

Dreamers were very rare and special. They were androgynous, opposites, paradoxical, translucent, very light, and appeared both young and yet old. Most importantly, they could manifest your dreams for you.

Beyond the Dreamers' Garden, they were found in a gazebo. It is here you would go when they called for you, only when they were ready to receive you. You would have to be able to answer their questions correctly. Then they would close their eyes in deep and wondrous sleep and would Dream your Dream into reality.

Lemuria is this land your imagination forgot!

Spark your own imagination to cross the terrain and travel on a quest to find a Dreamer. You too can ask the Dreamer to dream your dreams into existence, manifesting in physical time and space, not in Lemuria, but into our world, our reality.

If you are ready to rise above all thoughts, feelings and emotions you have created, then cross the Bridge of Beliefs and journey to the interior of Lemuria and to the Dreamer.

You can ask him or her to:

> *Dream me to dream my own living dream to come true, to awaken my dreams, by building my own dream with help and aid of the Lemurian Dreamer.*

Call to have special dreams come true without limits.

What Is Lemuria?

It is in the God/Goddess realm of your imagination. It exists beyond the Bridge of Beliefs. It is the land our imagination has forgotten. It may never be proven in black and white but exists nonetheless. To enter, we must rise above reason, thoughts, feelings and emotions and move into nonlinear experience. Here we travel beyond the Bridge of Beliefs to discover God/Goddess/All That Is.

Only when we are brave enough and courageous enough to suspend our physical illusion and cross over that bridge into the metaphysical can we find the land that our imagination has forgotten and find the land of the Dreamer.

One of the most important attributes of Lemuria is dreaming. In illusion, nothing is Real until you make it Real! It becomes real when you give it dimension, time and space.

Watch and look for the changes within your life. There is something deep inside our unconscious that has lain dormant, but it is stirring. Because it is in your unconscious, it may not express itself as "I remember Lemuria." It can come in as part of your creativity.

One day you may feel so satisfied and excited as you experience the realization that "This is I, becoming more! I have found something I forgot." A great joy and mystery is unfolding as you are living your life. This magic will become more real when we let it be "Real" that Lemuria is "Real"!

Lemuria is a land—yet it is much more. It is a state of Mind, of Being. When we are in our "Grace" we can become so much more. Choose to reflect, give attention, change how you act, change how you imagine yourself, and let it be "Real."

Lemurian Formula for Success:

Start with Love and end with Love.

Be conscious of your imagination.

Feel your love, and love for others.

The energy of Lemuria inside us is waiting to rise up. You will know when that happens because your heart will answer your questions.

Lemuria rising is about activating and raising the Lemurian energy within your new blue-green chakra, so you speak without anger or fear. This is an evolutionary process, just as it was in Lemuria.

We will learn to raise our heart energy to the same level of understanding of love and light that the Lemurians experienced in their times. At that point, our journey of moving from Fear to Love will be replaced with moving into more Love and Light. We will embrace our Lemurian energy and help change the world.

DNA plays a role in this journey of raising Lemurian energy. When we move into the fourth dimension we will have four strands of DNA vibrating. The fourth strand is golden. Fourth-dimensional people live through their Lemurian energy. They glow around their ears and the tops of their heads, much like Master Jesus did. As of 2010, Lemuria exists in the fifth-dimensional frequencies.

Be aware that your body is now radiating from inside your Heart Chakra, not only your physical heart. We must speak to our DNA through Intention in order to shut sickness off. We turned the sickness on, so now we must turn it off.

Our bodies connect to the love in our Heart Chakra, which lies underneath our emotional, mental and physical bodies. Our love resides in a blue-green heart chakra, the main force in this journey, because that is the only place our love is safe from our actions in the world.

Our emotions permeate others and the surrounding energy. Physical appearance is not important. Understand that our physical appearance is a projection of our understanding of this third-dimensional journey.

Our Heart Chakra is filled with pure love and light. It doesn't get angry. When a person experiences anger, the Heart Chakra pulls itself in tighter. So if you go home to a raging partner, just raise your heart energy! If you feel love, that's all you need! Your heart never falters.

Lemurian History

Mt. Shasta is not only the present home of the Lemurians, but it is also an interplanetary and intergalactic multidimensional portal. There is a huge etheric city of Light above the Mountain called the "Crystal City of Light of the Seven Rays."

This city is destined to be lowered onto our physical realm and become the first city of Light to manifest tangibly on the surface of this planet. In order for this to happen, the people who live here will have to match this vibration in their consciousness.

The Lemurian Age is said to have been from 4,500,000 BC to 12,000 BC.

Lemurians lived in a fifth-dimensional frequency and could switch back and forth from the fifth to the third at will without any problem. It could be done whenever it was desired by the intention of the heart energies.

The Lemurian Race was a mix of beings that came mainly from the star systems of Sirius and Alpha Centauri. My two ET contactees are from Alpha Centauri. Lemuria was really the cradle of civilization on the planet, the "Motherland" that assisted in the eventual birth of many other civilizations. Atlantis came about at a later time. Lemuria thrived in a state of Paradise and Magic for a few million years.

As a result of wars between the two major continents, great devastations took place. Lemuria and Atlantis battled over "ideologies." Lemurians believed less evolved cultures should be left alone to continue their own evolution at their own pace, according to their own understandings and pathways.

Atlantis believed the less evolved cultures should be brought under sway and controlled by the two more evolved civilizations. This caused a series of thermonuclear wars between Atlantis and Lemuria. There were no winners, and the people of the priesthood were informed that within less than 15,000 years their continents would sink completely. People in these civilizations lived an average of 20,000 to 30,000 years. Atlantis sank 200 years after the sinking of Lemuria.

Adama, the High Priest of Telos, he says, "There are seven major continents, and the continent of Lemuria includes land under the Pacific Ocean as well as Hawaii, Easter Island, Fiji, Australia and New Zealand, also land in the Indian Ocean and Madagascar, extended east to California and part of British Columbia."

California was part of the Lemurian land. When their civilization became threatened, the Lemurians petitioned Shambhala the Lesser, the head of the Agartha Network, for permission to build a city beneath Mt. Shasta in order to preserve their culture and records.

In order for the permission to be granted for Lemuria to become part of the subterranean Agartha Network, they had to prove to many, such as the Galactic Confederation of planets, that they had learned their lessons of war and aggression. They had to prove they had learned the lessons of "Peace" to become members of the Confederation.

Permission was granted—there was already a large dome cavern existing within Mt. Shasta. They called their city Telos.

There are five levels in the city. My favorite levels are the first and fifth. The First Level, where a large percentage of people live beneath the dome, houses several temples. The main temple of Ma Ra has a pyramid shape and is dedicated to the priesthood of Melchizedek. The pyramid is white, with the capstone, called the "living stone," donated to us from Venus.

The Fifth Level it is totally consecrated to nature. Tall trees, lakes, parks, and all the animals live here. In this nature level, many plants and animals have been preserved that are no longer on the Earth's surface. Animals are all vegetarians and do not eat each other.

All live side by side in total harmony, without fear and without any aggression towards people or towards each other. Telos is really the place where "the Lion and the Lamb lie side by side" and sleep together in total confidence.

Telos was also the name of this whole area at this time, including California and a major part of the southwest United States, as well as land north of Mt. Shasta along the west coast up to part of British Columbia.

It is interesting how I lived in these facets of Lemuria, feeling the connection in these areas. I lived on the coast of California and Oregon, in Point Arena and Crescent City in California and in Brookings in, Oregon. I also lived inland in Red Bluff and Redding near Mt. Shasta, the areas where Big Foot roamed. When I am in Sedona, my heart feels a dolphin connection; they lived in this area when it was an ocean. The most remembered of all the places I have lived is here in Kona, Hawaii, where I now live and play with my special friends, the dolphins. This is Lemuria!

"Telos" means, "Communicating with Spirit, Oneness with Spirit, Understanding with Spirit."

Adama says, "Only 25,000 people made it into the Mountain and were saved. This was what was left of the Lemurian culture on the third dimension." The blast came earlier than expected and the "Motherland" went down overnight. It came so quickly that everyone was unaware of what was happening. Practically all were sleeping. There were no unusual weather conditions. It was a nice, starry night.

A great part of the Priesthood remained faithful to the "Light" and their sacred calling, fearless to the end. They sang and prayed as they went down beneath the waves.

The melody they sang was "Auld Lang Syne." Through this action and sacrifice, choosing to stay together in groups and singing to the very end, much fear was mitigated and a certain level of harmony was maintained. Trauma and damage to the "souls" was greatly diminished for the souls who perished on that starry night.

The idea behind this action is that every horrifying experience leaves a deep traumatic scar in the etheric body, causing cellular memory that takes several embodiments to heal.

I remember being one that sang "Auld Lang Syne" as we were submerging beneath the waves. I shape-shifted or teleported immediately into the fourth-dimensional frequency where Lemuria had been lifted.

Auld Lang Syne was the last song ever heard on the land of Lemuria. "Should Auld Acquaintances Be Forgot?" We are these old acquaintances reuniting again, those of us from the physical realm with those of our beloved Lemurian realm. Our friends and family members of Telos are still "yet invisible" to our present sight. Physically, the veils are dropping and hopefully we will commune together soon.

Before beloved Lemuria sank completely, it was prophesized that one day, in a far and distant future, many of us will gather again as a group and sing this song again with the absolute knowingness that "Earth's Victory" is won. The time we are now living brings the "Celebration" of this long-awaited day and the fulfillment of that incredible prophecy. We are now initiating the beginning of the Re-Union!

In Telos, a main focus has been to hold the energies of Ascension Consciousness for the planet until such a time that surface dwellers can do this for themselves. Now the time has come for our two civilizations to merge together as "ONE HEART"! As our Consciousness rises, a memory is activated in each of us. It simply takes the form of your own spiritual and inner wisdom.

The ancients never had a religion and never felt the need to make someone else believe the way they did. This is another connection that I remember. Despite being baptized, as was typical in my youth, I was never made to go to church. I would only go on special occasions with friends.

As a child I never felt comfortable when the minister began speaking. I was very intuitive and knew his words weren't in alignment with what he was really thinking. It didn't feel real to me. I seemed to have the gift of knowing what people were really thinking. So I never had a religion, and, being Lemurian, I didn't need a religion: Nature was my inspiration!

The Lemurians who live in Telos are described as graceful and tall, seven to eight feet or more, with long flowing hair. They dress in white robes and sandals, although they have also been seen in colorful clothing. Their slender bodies are adorned with decorative collars of beads or precious stones.

The light inside the Mountain is as bright as a summer's day. Suspended almost in the center of that great cavern of space is a giant glowing mass of light. The Lemurians control most of their technology with their minds.

"The Little People of Mt. Shasta," as they are often referred to, are still here in physical immortal bodies, totally unlimited, living a life of pure Heaven on Earth. They are often seen visually around the Mountain.

THE NEW LEMURIA

Lemuria has never been totally destroyed. It still exists to this day in a fourth- and fifth-dimensional frequency, not yet visible to our third-dimensional vision and perception. The veil continues to lift and become thinner. In a not-too-distant future, beloved Lemuria will emerge in Her New Splendor and Glory and reveal Herself to you in a very physical and tangible way.

As we open ourselves to a higher conscious way of living and purify ourselves of all distorted belief systems, we will be able to perceive our beloved "Motherland" once again.

At the time of the blast, Lemuria lifted into a fourth-dimensional frequency. It continued to thrive and evolve to the level of perfection and beauty it has now reached.

Those of Telos ask you to connect with them through love, openly heart-to-heart. Ask for their assistance and they will be with you, as you do this most important inner work. The people in Telos are very eager to assist all those who will reach out to them. They are a civilization that has achieved great heart openings, and their vibration pulses with the Heart of the Divine Mother.

The New Day, the New World is just about to be born and unfold again its learned lessons of Love.

The Lemurians who remained faithful to the Light and Her sacred calling were lifted up to the fourth dimension at the time of the cataclysm. Lemuria exists fully in the higher dimension. Crystals associated with pyramids are a Diamond Energy Power Source at the core. The diamonds associated with these pyramids have one facet, which is perfect for the Lemurian journey. As we move into the fourth dimension, these diamond crystals will be the basis of the journey. All power sources will be run through these diamond energies.

My home is filled with crystals. I have always had a passion for crystals, whether wearing them or enjoying their company in my home. We communicate Being-to-Being, assisting each other in so many ways. They are my pure, true, living friends of high vibrational energies.

Chapter 2

First Awakenings

In my childhood years, growing up in Pt. Arena, California, I had to work on being more grounded and physical. I can remember being first grade, watching the other children play and trying to see what this game of life was all about! Up until my early school years I kept to myself, wandering on our land, communicating with the many animals that lived on our farm. This was my "joy" in life: to be in nature and on the land with the animals.

In this particular lifeline I was born into a strong Norwegian/Swedish ancestry. I knew in this life that I would have to have a strong foundation in order for me to stay more grounded compared with the realm of the Angels from which I originate. I was given a very grounded Norwegian name, Margie. I loved my family, yet when I was very young I would look up at the stars and wonder what I was doing here.

I remember my favorite cow. I was only three years old when, unfortunately, a mother cow passed away while giving birth. Still, she left a beautiful calf. Every day my dad and I would bottle-feed her so she could eat. This was my passion, each morning to go out with Dad and feed our little calf! I was so little that when the calf would butt the bottle, I would start laughing and almost fall over. I still remember how much fun I would have. It was an especially wonderful time my dad and I shared together.

Eventually my sweet little calf turned into a very large cow. I have pictures of me sitting atop this huge cow, looking like a tiny little dot upon her. We were wonderful friends, until one day she was gone.

Living on a farm, sometimes life can seem very cruel, especially when you are a child that fed a calf as a friend. To discover one day that this beloved animal would become food for the family was a very sad experience.

My dad was so very kind and gentle with me, knowing how sensitive I was even as a child. He always did his best not to let me see the more harsh side of life living on a farm. This was especially true in a small coastal town back in the 1950s.

This was my first experience of grief and shock; I was heartbroken by what I saw. My dad told me not to come wandering in our back yard, a large open space behind the house without fencing. But, being who I was, even at three years old, with an insatiable curiosity, of course I had to sneak out back to see why I wasn't supposed to go! To my shock, there was hanging from one of our large trees my dear friend, the cow I had fed as a calf.

You may have guessed I do not eat meat. It has always saddened me to think that I could eat an animal, especially one that I saw grow up so strong and happy. I still do not eat any red meat, yet I am aware that in times past, and even still,(?) animals have and do sacrifice their lives for humans as food if the humans' survival is at stake.

Being a lover of ALL animals, I do know there is a balance between living and dying, yet only when the animal and the person can have the highest communication and respect for each other. Before an animal relinquishes its life to the person whose life it will enhance for nourishment, a ritual must be shared between both, as long as it is the highest good for both animal and human.

I don't believe in going out and killing animals for pleasure, and today even killing animals for food isn't as necessary for people to survive as it was when I was growing up. It's a fine line, and I do prefer that all animals and humans live together in peace and harmony without having to take lives of these precious ones.

For me, the Lemurian Way of Life is to revere all the animals! To share space and time with them in loving communion and communication. This is the highest form of unconditional love.

Thus, I feel very strongly about the killing of our dolphins, whales, and all the cetaceans with the violent methods that are being used at present. It is sad and it breaks my heart to think we are killing these conscious, loving, gentle higher species of animals.

Living on the coast of Point Arena near Fort Bragg was very beautiful. I learned a deep respect for the ocean with its mysterious lore. My dad had an old book called *Moby Dick*, and when he let me see the book I claimed it for myself! I kept it by my bed and each night before I would go to sleep I would hold it and look through it, even though I couldn't read the words. It really only had very few pictures, so why was I so fascinated by this book about a whale and its experience with humans?

This was really my beginning of communicating with the whales; I didn't even realize it until I started working with the whales and dolphins years later! All I knew is that I would fall asleep in the comfort of this whale, my friend of the sea!

I have always been in the healing profession, the focus of helping others. Even as a young girl in grade school I was chosen to help others when they needed assistance. I was sent to bring all new students around to introduce them to our peers. They seemed to feel safe with me. People would just tell me things, saying, "I am not sure why I am telling you this!"

I would find myself in places many times where assistance was needed very quickly in that moment. In these moments I never questioned "Why is this happening? Why am I here?" I knew I was in the right place at the right time, always having the skill that was needed at the time.

I then began to see that I did have some kind of a special gift that made others feel very comfortable; my presence seemed to be uplifting to them.

Angel and Fairy Realms

When I was three years old, beloved angels and fairies taught me to communicate with them through my dolls. In hindsight, it was ingenious way of connecting to Source and angels without feeling I was doing something wrong, something I shouldn't be doing!

My older brothers teased me because I was always talking to my angels. Since they couldn't see them, they thought I was talking to myself. They didn't know I was really talking with angels and fairies. After learning what I needed to do, I could talk with them any time I wanted.

I could do this without people questioning, "whom I was talking to"—something that often happens with children who have unseen friends. These children are usually criticized and stop communicating with their friends. In my case, I had many dolls and would talk to my angelic friends through them.

But as I got older and less conversational with my dolls, I shut down my communication for a period of time as I was trying to fit in with my peers. Much later when I got married, this continued further as I shut down my inner communications. My husband wasn't sure it was OK to speak about things he couldn't observe in his reality. It took many years until I could begin again to be more of MYSELF versus WHO I WAS SUPPOSED TO BE!

The angels told me I they would always be with me. All I would have to do is ask them for guidance whenever I needed help, and they would be with me. If I needed clarification about something that was troubling me, they would be with me. If I felt lonely, they said to ask them to come and we could talk, for we were friends, especially when I was younger. They were my best friends. They said, "You will never be alone. We are always watching over you. Remember you too are also an angel!"

Around age five, I was able to wander outside around our house to commune with the nature spirits, divas and fairies. This seemed to fulfill my curiosity and appetite for the outdoors. We had land with lots of trees where the nature spirits lived. I realized I could communicate with these special friends and thought everyone communicated with them. When I got a little older I saw that people didn't know what I was talking about or looked at me strangely if I spoke about the divas and fairies.

I loved the freedom of wandering by myself, daydreaming as children do. I was never disturbed and there wasn't anyone around, just nature and myself. Oh, I loved those carefree days!

Unexpected things were also happening. It wasn't unusual for me at times to be found downstairs, in the middle of the night wandering around sleepwalking, yet never remember getting there.

One night I was drawn to go downstairs by a window. I remember looking out and seeing a UFO. It was a bright light and it felt like I was communicating with it. I only remember that little bit. I'm not sure how I even got back in bed, yet it felt like a long period of time had gone by. During these events I was around four or five years old. I believe I was having positive ET contact in my early childhood. Since then, I sense and feel energies very easily.

I was always very sensitive to energies in the homes I lived, especially the older homes. Around this same time I began to have nightmares, feeling a presence in the room. I would call for one of my brothers, who would come and get in bed with me, and I would go back to sleep.

We moved to Red Bluff when I started fourth grade. My room was next to my brother's. I started immediately feeling a presence in my room; it was very scary to me. My dad would come in and say there was nothing there. It would stop for a while, and then happen again. After my brother graduated, I moved into his room. The same thing started again. The wall separated my parents' room and my room and there would be times when I would freeze with fear. All I could do was to knock on the wall so my dad would come in. Again he would come and reassure me nothing was there. It finally got so bad that I was moved into my parents' room for a while so everyone could sleep. I eventually was moved back to my room and all seemed to be OK.

I do know there was a spirit in our house. It stopped scaring me at night, but there would be times when I would be walking down the hall and I could feel someone walking behind me. I'd turn around and no one was there! We found out later that the grandmother of the family who owned the house before us had died in my room. I guess she wasn't ready to leave.

I had one other spirit contact me in a very old house we bought and remodeled in Susanville. We had a basement and it was very scary to go down there, especially one area that was open earth, resembling a dugout. Whenever I would pass this area I would hurry; it was cold and it gave me eerie feelings. I would finish my task quickly and get out as fast as I could. As I reached the top of the stairs it would feel as though someone were coming up the stairs after me.

I started not going down there so much, but then this spirit started coming into the kitchen from up the stairs. Several times I would be fixing something and I could feel it watching me, standing at the doorway. One day I got so tired of it I said, "Leave now!" To my surprise it did. Many times I would see a wisp of energy moving near me. The scariest time was when I was in the showerand I felt and saw a shadow pass by the glass shower door. I yelled at it to stop! Thankfully, this was the last time it disturbed me and we sold the house shortly after.

Sixth-Dimensional Guides, Big Foot

Big Foot was the name they were called in northern California where I grew up. I referred to them as my sixth-dimensional special guides from early childhood to today. They are beautiful beings that are here to assist in our evolution.

I remember staying with a friend when I was five years old who lived in the redwood forest. This was the first time I had ever stayed overnight with anyone other than my family. We were walking in the forest and could feel a larger presence in the trees. It was something I had never experienced before. It wasn't frightening, yet it was a very different energy and a little confusing to me. I loved the forest and felt safe, despite the feeling of this unusual presence that seemed to be following close.

That night I couldn't sleep and while in my bed I could feel this same presence surround me. It was an intense energy, yet at the same time it felt loving and gentle. I didn't know at the time that this was the first time I was experiencing my "Sixth-Dimensional Group of Big Foot." They were able to manifest themselves from the sixth dimension to the third dimension at will.

Since I was so young they would come and surround me with "LOVE" to let me know that they were there and would always protect me from any harm. If they were to materialize at that age it would have been a shock to me and we both knew that.

I had several years of contact with them but never in physical form until one incredible experience when I was 18 years old. Late one night after returning from a date, I was in the kitchen making something to eat when I heard an indescribable, out-of-this-world, high-pitch, sonar sound. It literally froze me. I had never heard anything like it before.

I hadn't yet met my dolphin and whale friends, so wasn't familiar at that time with high-pitch sonic sounds. I felt a huge presence outside our picture window looking at me. I wasn't frightening for some reason, so I relaxed and felt amazing love transmitting from this presence. It was sending a love vibration at a cellular level, into the core of my being!

I turned around and nothing was there. The presence and feelings were gone as if it had never happened. I turned back and continued to make my snack and went to bed without another thought of what had just happened. How was that possible?

It really felt very loving and gentle with a BIG Energy! It is similar to when I swim with the humpback whales: very loving, nurturing and gentle, yet has a huge presence of Being.

The next morning, my boyfriend and soon-to -be husband came out and said he was following reporters down to the diversion dam pass near where I lived. He said that someone had made tracks of Big Foot.

"Oh, my God," I said, and in that moment I remembered the night before and my contact with the "not-from-this-world" sound and presence. I told him my experience the night before. Please understand where we were living in Red Bluff was a very conservative town. Even though we all grew up knowing Big Foot roamed the foothills, we didn't know they would go to someone's home and say, "Hi, I am here!"

He couldn't believe it could be possible and more or less looked at me as if I was having a bad day. I knew the best thing for me was to drop the matter, knowing I knew the truth of what I had heard and experienced. That was all that really mattered.

I had to learn this way of living early in my childhood and adulthood because of mystical experiences throughout my life. I learned later why my memory had been wiped clear that evening. It is their way of not adding stress to my life or overloading my circuits depending on where I am emotionally at the time.

We lived in Big Foot country, yet so many still couldn't believe that they were real; even when they had been briefly spotted only to disappear right in front of people. Big Foot had also turned over many bulldozers in the foothills where the logging of trees took place. People would even see footprints of Big Foot and wonder how the equipment could get turned over, still saying it isn't possible!

It was as if their consciousness would not go there. Little did they know of our multi-dimensional brothers and sisters. They were and are very real. It's normal to experience their presence often in many places where I have lived, even places others wouldn't believe they could be. I am blessed to have them in my life, without fear, knowing I love them as much as they love me.

When they first come into a space I can feel them. They let you know they are present, yet sometimes in the next moment it is like the slate is wped clean! I would forget and resume what I was doing before the experience. (This happens only once in a while.) Then I have a reminder; something will spark my attention to remembering the experience. It is almost like I am remembering that I am Lemurian and have had sparks of remembering my entire life.

I can see now how they present their energies gently, so as not to scare me. More importantly, it allows me to get used to their higher frequency and lets it blend more with my own frequency.

They alter time and space with me after the initial contact in my field. Actually, my memory is stored away for a future time to remember. I have forgotten only minutes later the feelings and information that has been shared with me. How would one forget such wonderful feelings of love and knowing, to remember in a future time?

All I know is a wonderful feeling of love and compassion that will always be with me, as if it happened only yesterday. I truly look forward to more contact on a regular basis with my ET friends, dolphins, whales, angels, and all beings of light from the Heavenly realms of love and light.

Oregon Big Foot

My husband and I moved to Oregon in 1986 and we lived three miles from the Redwood forest. Each day I would walk my two dogs on the logging trails. We were being greeted by my Big Foot friends on many walks.

They didn't always manifest into physical reality; however, they would let me know when they were present. For example, one day I was walking along a trail near a creek, when suddenly it was as if I had walked into a "vortex." All sounds stopped: no more singing birds or the sound of the gentle winds! I could see my dogs outside of this vortex, myself still within the bubble of energy. I am not sure how long I was in the bubble of love, as I was well accustomed to how time bends during these experiences.

Once again I started to walk, hearing birds chirping and feeling the gentle breezes upon my face. Something told me to turn around, and as I did I looked into the bushes to see the branches swaying back and forth quickly, as if someone was walking through them. No one was there, no surprise to me, as I knew they were present without showing themselves visibly.

The group of Big Foot sent me the message that they were there with me by showing me the movements of the trees. The love was so pure and light. It was wonderful to share time with my beloved friends.

After the dogs and I would have our sacred walks in the forest, I would drive into Brookings, which was three miles to the ocean. Here we would walk along the long beautiful, white crystalline beaches by the shoreline, just like the Lemuria I remembered! We could walk for miles never seeing anyone; it was amazing to have been blessed to live between the redwoods and the ocean only a few minutes away.

Later we moved into Brookings and lived in the oldest Victorian home in town. It had a view of the ocean and harbor. What a wonderful experience while we lived there, even though the fog was chilling cold at times. This was so familiar, I know when I would experience these adventures I was in the fifth dimension, experiencing living in Lemuria, and I would remember I was Lemurian. These vortexes were familiar to me. The first time I really remembered being taken into one was when I attended an Angelic seminar by Santa Rosa on the coast. I was walking a trail on lunch break into a beautiful and sunny area surrounded by redwoods. There was a moment when Big Foot created a vortex for me to enter. I stepped into this incredible space of no time/no space, and as I did, all sounds of the birds or wind stopped. It was pure silence and a feeling of peaceful serenity was gently embracing the moment with love and light.

Big Foot in Hawaii
Assistance with a Serious Challenge

I had moved to the Big Island. One sunny, beautiful day while walking a sacred trail, to my surprise I passed an area feeling like someone was communicating with me. An energy reached out to me as I was walking past a very sacred place.

I stopped to feel what I was experiencing, and to my excitement, it was the same energy I felt in Oregon! Oh, I was filled with such love, joy and bliss; it was my Big Foot friends here in Hawaii! How could that be—did they come here, or were they always with me no matter where I was living?

I quickly got my answer. They said:

WE HAVE ALWAYS BEEN WITH YOU SINCE YOU WERE THREE YEARS OLD WHEN THE LARGER PART OF YOU DESCENDED INTO YOUR VERY SMALL BODY THE NIGHT YOU HAD A HIGH FEVER. THIS IS WHEN YOU TRANSITIONED INTO YOUR LEMURIAN BODY SO YOU WOULD BE ABLE TO MOVE THROUGH LIFE A LITTLE EASIER. YOU KNEW THERE WOULD BE SOME CHALLENGING TIMES AHEAD. YOU WOULD KNOW WHAT TO DO WITH YOUR ENERGY BODY AND MOVE QUICKLY THROUGH THESE EXPERIENCES BY REMEMBERING LEMURIA, YOUR ORIGINAL BLUEPRINT WHEN YOU CAME INTO THIS TIMELINE.

I was facing an unfortunate situation in my life that required immediate medical attention. I tried to speak with a doctor and make an appointment to be seen; yet the one doctor recommended to me was on vacation and the other doctor I couldn't see for several days ahead.

The receptionist didn't understand the seriousness of my condition. I was so frustrated that I took a walk to my sacred area and I felt the energies more intense than ever being projected toward me, trying to communicate to me. I was so upset I didn't pay attention and kept walking to where I loved spending time: on the lava near the water.

Once I got to my special place, I walked out to the edge and yelled out, "Please help me!" I immediately got an answer saying, "Go home and call the doctor."

I thought it was my angelic guides for it was such a familiar feeling of love. The message was to go home right now and call, so I quickly headed back so that I could do what they had told me to do.

The doctor I called happened to be the one that was on vacation, yet I knew it was this doctor that I had to call, even knowing he wasn't supposed to be there. I called anyway and his receptionist answered.

I told her my situation and she said that the doctor had just arrived back and had stopped into the office. He said for me to come into his office right away. After seeing me, I was scheduled for surgery that next morning, knowing I needed immediate attention.

This proved to me that when you ask for help it is there for you! Instead of my angels responding, it was my Big Foot guides that gave me the message. They were the ones trying to communicate with me as I passed the sacred site. If I had paid attention and stopped and listened, I believe I would have gotten the message at that time. They saved my life in many ways; if my condition had been left longer without medical attention it could have been very serious.

I would have never received this message if I hadn't asked for help. The amazing part of the story is how did they know the doctor had arrived back to Kona? They knew and responded to my request knowing how scared and frustrated I felt. I was thinking no one was listening, and here they were sending this wonderful doctor to take care of me! All we need to do is ask and we shall receive if we are open and listening!

My Big Foot guides having been with me since I can remember, at least from the age of five when I first experienced their presence. They told me: WE ARE THE ONES YOU SAW BEFORE YOU FELL ASLEEP. WE WANTED YOU TO KNOW THAT YOU WERE NOT ALONE, WE WERE WATCHING OVER YOU AS YOU SLEPT EACH NIGHT. WE WERE PROTECTING YOU FROM SOME INFLUENCES THAT WERE PRESENT IN THE HOUSE THAT COULD HAVE DISTURBED YOU NEEDLESSLY. WE ARE SORRY WE SCARED YOU AT FIRST WHEN YOU SAW OUR FACES. REMEMBER YOU WOULD FALL ASLEEP HOLDING YOUR TEDDY BEAR FOR COMFORT. IT LOOKED LIKE THE CLOSEST THING TO WHAT WE LOOKED LIKE BECAUSE YOU HADN'T SEEN US PHYSICALLY. THE TEDDY BEAR REPRESENTED US. WE WILL BE WITH YOU THROUGHOUT THIS EARTHLY EXPERIENCE ASSISTING YOU WHENEVER YOU REQUIRE OUR PRESENCE. WE LOVE YOU DEARLY.

I had started swimming with the dolphins every day, journaling my daily experiences. The dolphins were my gift from the Lemurians, as were my Big Foot friends and the Angels. From that point on, the Angels (my first playmates), Big Foot, Dolphins and Whales have been guiding me, like Lemurian friends. We would spend the rest of our lives in constant communication! I can't tell you how blessed I am to know and experience such wonderful loving beings of light and love.

Chapter 3

Animal Blessings

So many animals have helped me through traumatic times in my life. One animal influence stands out above all: my precious dogs! I can't remember one moment of sadness that they were not there to console me. They listened and were present to my every need. What I love about dogs is that they are so unconditionally loving and help us to feel more balanced, if we allow ourselves to share our lives with them.

When I was young, my dad had asthma and would have an attack when too close to dogs. I always wanted them to sleep with me and be near me, yet while living at home they had to be outside. That was so hard for me. I didn't like seeing my dad feel bad, so I accepted what was.

My brother had a dog and when we moved from Point Arena to Red Bluff, Bootsie, our dog, came with us. He lived for a few years and when Bootsie died my dad did get another dog. We lived in the country close to the road, and shortly after he was hit by a car. My dad then said we couldn't have any more dogs. Wow, that was hard being the animal lover and not having a dog. It was what had to be.

My dad surprised me with a horse when I was in fifth grade. I called him Brownie. He took my mind off not having a dog. I rode Brownie every day after school and it was great fun. When I turned sixteen my dad said I could get a car so I could drive back and forth to school so I didn't have to ride the bus. The problem was I would have to sell Brownie to help pay for a car. At first I was sad, yet being sixteen and heavily involved in school activities, choosing the car was the best choice for me at that time.

It wasn't until I got married that I had my very own dog! My next wonderful furry friend was a German Shepherd/Wolf mix who I called Buddy.

I was so happy! It was wonderful. Buddy could come in the house. We had moved from my hometown and Dad was only able to visit once in a while. When he did visit, I would make sure Buddy stayed in the garage. It worked out very nicely; I loved them both and knew there would be a way for us all to enjoy ourselves.

Buddy lived a wonderful life and passed on. Then I saw an advertisement for free puppies. When I went into the owner's garage there were so many puppies I didn't know which one to pick! I love white dogs and there was a little white one in the group. I asked that I be guided to the one that was supposed to come home with me. To my surprise it wasn't the white pup; another pup came straight to me and into my open arms as I sat on the floor. This was the one! I named him Nickie. He, like Buddy, was a mix of German Shepherd/Wolf and he too was always by my side, always protective of me.

One sad day came when Nickie could no longer get up, so I made the heartwrenching decision to help him go in peace. Before my husband took him to the vet, I connected to Nickie and told him if he chose to come back to me in another dog I would love it and that I would know it was him/her by the eyes! I cried for days. A good friend surprised me with a beautiful painting of Nickie that she had painted from a photo I had and have still.

Next, I found the cutest puppy in a box outside of Safeway. I brought him home and he said to call him Babaji. He became my court jester since his behavior always made me laugh, which was greatly needed.

One day while in the yard I had a feeling that I needed to go to town, into Auburn. I didn't travel the canyon road from Cool, California unless I had a list of things to do, but I changed clothes, and, without a list, I headed for town. I wasn't sure where I was going; all I knew was that I was driving towards town. Instead of stopping in town I continued until I found myself at the Humane Society. Could it be that Nickie had come back as my new puppy?

One of the kennels had the same mix breed as my Nickie, and again there were so many puppies. I saw a white one but I didn't want to just say I'd take him because he was white. I went outside walking around and said to myself, "The one that comes to me first is the one that is meant for me."

I felt one of them was Nickie, my sweet friend back again. I opened the door and sat down and oh my, this little white furry ball came up into my arms. I picked him up and looked him in the eyes, seeing his soul. It was my Nickie, he had returned to me again! I got my white dog and he told me his name was "Nickea."

When Nickea was three months old I asked an animal communicator to come over. As we were sitting in my bedroom where my beautiful painting of Nickie hung, she asked Nickea if he was Nickie returned.

To my amazement, he looked up at the painting of Nickie, then to me and to her! It was a special, incredible moment; my beloved dog was back with me again. I brought both Babaji and Nickea over to live in Hawaii with my husband and me. The dogs both loved Hawaii; the warm weather was very good for them.

Today I have two rescue dogs. When I wrote this I had a lovely black lab, Sheba. After thirteen years, I had to make a heartbreaking choice to lay her to rest. After the vet came and gave her the tranquilizer, he said that she had spinal damage, so I felt relieved that I had made the right choice for Sheba.

In her final beautiful moments, I had a few friends present and we placed Sheba in the living room on her blanket so she was comfortable and secure. We sat around her as the vet gave her the shot and she quietly passed into a place of Peace and Serenity.

My good friends made her a place to rest in my back yard that I can look down on from my lanai. I know this isn't where she really is, for I know she is overshadowing my new rescue puppy I adopted the same day: a seven-month-old chocolate lab/mix. I asked her what her name was, noticing that Mary Magdalene's energy was all around her and me.

I looked the puppy in the eye and she said "Magdalene!" It was a beautiful moment. I call her Maddie as a nickname. I am also very blessed to have Noel, my Christmas rescue doggie of three years. What joy they are.

Now I only rescue dogs. They need homes so they can receive loving hugs where they feel safe. Most rescue dogs have had trauma and need our help to be adopted and enjoy a loving home. Maddie is the first rescue that has come to me without lots of trauma. She and her mom were rescued when Maddie was only six weeks old.

So many animals need our help to give them love. They say dogs, dolphins and whales all come from the star system Sirius. This is why these are my favorite animals: because they match who I am.

Chapter 4

The Dolphins and Whales Help Us All

Impression of the author holding "Trusty," the baby dolphin. Artwork by Eva M. Sakmar-Sullivan

I feel that everyone ever introduced to the dolphins and whales has been shifted in many ways—whether they have had serious illnesses or have simply chosen to swim, play and enjoy themselves in the cetaceans' aquatic environment.

One beautiful example is when I took a woman who was in a wheelchair out to be with the dolphins. I had to pull her along with the assistance of a boogie board. She was paralyzed from the waist down. After our first trip, I noticed that she could use her walker better. After the second trip, she said she could walk around her hotel room unassisted. At the completion of our third day out with the dolphins, she walked from her room to the lobby, which was quite a distance. She came back the next year and experienced additional healing with the dolphins. Her life was forever changed!

Another precious example is a woman who journeyed on my first whale trip. She had lymphatic cancer and her medical team had advised her to have surgery. She chose to join my trip even though she was very weak. After spending time in the water enjoying intimate and close encounters with the whales, her energy and her immune system improved. Ultimately, she was able to live a better life.

We are all experiencing more and more changes, individually and collectively, on the earth plane. Let us bless and embrace these changes and know that no matter what we see in our third-dimensional reality, it is all in Divine Order in other dimensions. We have collectively asked for change, for a new era, and for a better world... and now we are in process!

I am so grateful to wake up every day in Hawaii, Lemuria, my Paradise! I transmit love and gratitude to you all from the center of my heart! Be and swim free! Live in love, light, harmony, and joy... always!

DOLPHIN MESSAGE:

WE ARE HERE TO HELP YOU EXPERIENCE THE HIGHER ESSENCE OF WHO YOU REALLY ARE: THE BEING WHO RESIDES INSIDE YOU, NOT ABOVE YOU LIKE YOU WOULD THINK, BUT YOUR TRUE ESSENCE OF LOVE, JOY AND COMPASSION. WE WOULD LIKE TO HAVE YOU LOOK INSIDE, TO SEE WHAT IS REALLY THERE AS WE SEE YOU. WE SEE YOU AS LOVING BEINGS WHO CAME ONTO THE PLANET AT THIS TIME TO ASSIST MOTHER EARTH AND ALL BEINGS UPON HER TO BECOME YOUR EVOLVED SELVES AS YOU ONCE WERE BEFORE YOU DECIDED TO EMBODY INTO THIS PHYSICAL PLANE OF EXISTENCE. WE SO LOVE YOU AND WISH FOR YOU TO SEE YOU AS YOU TRULY ARE: GREAT BEINGS AND ENTITIES CARRYING THE LIGHT AND LOVE THAT IS TRULY YOUR INHERITANCE. YOU HAVE COME TO SHARE THIS LIGHT AND LOVE AMONGST YOURSELVES, TO ASSIST EACH OTHER IN YOUR EVOLUTION. TODAY WE WERE SHOWING YOU HOW TO COME TOGETHER AS ONE ENTITY OF LIGHT AND LOVE AND THEN SPREAD THIS ENERGY TO EVERYONE AND EVERYTHING YOU COME INTO CONTACT WITH. THE BUBBLES ARE OUR WAY OF SHARING OUR JOY WITH YOU AND FOR OURSELVES, FOR WE RESIDE IN THE ENERGIES OF JOY AND PLAY. WE KNOW YOU KNOW THIS AND ARE SPENDING MORE TIME IN THESE FAMILIAR ENERGIES.

PLEASE SHARE YOUR JOY AND LAUGHTER WITH OTHERS, ESPECIALLY THOSE WHO NEED YOUR SMILE OF JOY SO THAT THEY CAN ALSO SEE THEY CARRY THIS INSIDE OF THEM. WE LOVE YOU. WE KNOW WHO YOU ARE AND ARE VERY PROUD OF WHAT YOU ARE DOING. WE KNOW YOU LOVE US EQUALLY AS WE LOVE YOU. UNTIL NEXT TIME, MAY YOU BE BLESSED WITH ALL THAT YOU SEE, AS IT IS ALL THAT YOU ARE! THE DOLPHINS

This is very touching as it seems these special message bubbles are becoming very important for us to assimilate into our knowingness. A few days after this message, I was at my favorite bay when a mother and her baby blew a bubble under me so I could easily move into it. It was more on the surface of the water instead of me diving into it. I asked, "Why did you blow the bubble on the surface of the water?"

MESSAGE: THIS BUBBLE WAS FOR YOU TO LOOK AT YOUR SURFACE BEHAVIOR ATTITUDES AT THIS TIME. WE SEE THAT THERE WERE SOME THOUGHTS THAT YOU HAVE BEEN CARRYING AROUND WITH YOU THAT WERE NO LONGER SERVING YOU. IT WAS TIME FOR THEM TO BE BURST OPEN AND BE DISSOLVED. WE SEE YOU HAVE COME TO TERMS WITH THE ISSUE OF YOUR OLD RELATIONSHIP, NEEDING TO SPEAK OF IT ONCE MORE FOR THE FINAL TIME. WE NOW SEE YOU ARE COMPLETE WITH THIS STORY. BE PATIENT AND STAY OPEN, NO NEED TO DIVE DEEPLY TO FIGURE THIS OUT.

Wow, I see the bubble message was about myself and my partner and the surface issue (bubble on the surface breaking). The two bubble rings I had to dive down into to go more deeply into were the frequencies of my old thoughts. I was able to see clearly: "who I am and who I am becoming"! What a blessed day in paradise again!

Sacred Moments of the Blue-Eyed Dolphin

I experienced a huge leap in my life towards becoming more of "Who I Am" on a trip to San Diego. Walking along the beach one day, I noticed five or six bottlenose dolphins riding in the waves. It was like seeing them through a clear, liquid waveform. I was amazed and it was as if no one else saw them. It felt like they were following me on my walk as they rode the wave. I reached the end of the beach and turned around to head back. To my surprise, they did the same thing! They followed me all the way back to my starting point!

The next day I spent hours at the aquatic park sitting with the whales and the dolphins. I returned for three days in a row and realized how easily I was communicating with my new friends. On the last day, I was down at the viewing window when this very large dolphin with a BLUE EYE connected with me. I knew what he was saying! I got so excited! For a moment I questioned his blue eye, thinking, "Dolphins don't have blue eyes, do they?" I asked the attendant about it and he said, "No, they don't have blue eyes!" Well, this one did. He came around many times looking into my eyes, and his eye was sky-blue!

I later asked why the blue-eyed dolphin had appeared to me and the answer was, "I AM HERE WITH YOU, MY SWEET DAUGHTER. ONE DAY YOU WILL LOVE AND WORK WITH THE DOLPHINS!

REMEMBER I SAID BEFORE MY PASSING: I WILL ALWAYS BE WITH YOU. I WILL NEVER LEAVE YOU!"

My dad had made his transition only months earlier and those were the words he said to me. I felt this was my dad's way of saying he is OK and that he loves me and wants me to be happy. This moment changed my life; my work was to be with the dolphins to help others to heal their challenges, as well as to enjoy spending time with dolphins in pure joy.

My dad had clear sky-blue eyes and, interestingly, I also had sky-blue eyes until a major shift occurred in my life at the age of three. After several days of running a high fever, my eye color changed from blue to hazel-brown. Some people call this "soul braiding."

Upon arriving home, there was a message from my friend asking if I wanted to go to Hawaii to swim with the dolphins! This was Divine Intervention! A week later I found myself in Hawaii attending a dolphin seminar with Doug Hackett and Trish Regan, who became my very best friends. I was one of three participants in their very first seminar. Before leaving, my friend who is a 12th-dimensional psychic reader said, "A dolphin is going to take you through all 12 dimensions of time!" I responded just as quickly, "Oh yes, I know!" How did I know this?

The real excitement was just beginning! I had never snorkeled or swum in the ocean before. It was the first or second day out in the water, when one dolphin left the pod and swam over to me. I knew this was the Master Dolphin who was to be my teacher. I knew I would be taken through all 12 dimensions of time. All was going as planned. This beautiful, amazing dolphin and I swam for who knows how long, eye-to-eye, embracing each other with so much love.

I experienced a connection of peace, serenity, pure joy of heart like I had never felt before! I remember many different sensations taking place within my body, mind and spirit. What I wasn't aware of was that I had become invisible to my swim partner Lisa! I knew I was shifting from one sensation to another, but didn't know I was invisible. I could see the other swimmers the entire time.

The most serene and familiar sensation that registered as I went through all 12 dimensions was comparable to the realm where Big Foot, my sixth-dimensional group of guides, had taken me several times during our encounters. It is an environment of total peace and quietude, a suspended dimension of "no time, no space." This continues today as I swim with my beloved dolphin friends, weaving in and out of "no time, no space," disappearing within our intimate connections.

During my dolphin-induced initiation to the 12 dimensions of time, neither Lisa nor the other swimmers were able to see me. My energy signature was raised so high that I disappeared! Lisa panicked, wondering where I had gone. She searched for me, thinking she would be able to easily see me in my hot-pink bathing suit, snorkel, mask and fins. Why couldn't I be seen?

Eventually the dolphins told me to go to shore. I walked out of the water, looked right at Lisa and said, "Hey Lisa, what's up?" Her eyes became as big as saucers. She asked how I had gotten out of the water. I replied, "I walked out." She asked again and I could see she wasn't kidding. I quickly got the message from the dolphins that until I spoke, I had been completely invisible to her. Wow, very interesting!

The next day Trish asked me to let her know if the same dolphin I had connected with appeared. And guess what, he did! I motioned Trish over, we locked arms, and he approached the same way as the previous day. Other swimmers were watching to see what would happen. This time, we both became invisible! Not bad for my first swim with the dolphins and a first-time snorkeler.

The dolphins asked me to be a steward for them, a way-shower, to bring people to learn, share, heal, play, and enjoy themselves in their presence. The dolphins love us as much as we love them; it is a mutual sharing of love and light that is exchanged when we swim together.

What a healing we all shared! We learned how the dolphins could assist us in elevating our frequencies to shift our cells to embody Love, Light and Joy. I decided that this was to be my life's work. After five years of speaking about the dolphins and bringing people to Hawaii to swim and share in their Essence, I was given the opportunity to move to the island. I am so appreciative that Hank, my former husband, supported me that first year as I spent every day swimming with the dolphins and journaling my experiences without having to worry about anything else.

"Trusty," Healing of a Baby Dolphin: My Way of Giving Back

In June 2001, while assisting a swim participant and sending out my signature tones to the dolphins, I noticed a baby dolphin approaching me. Instead of stopping, he very gently tapped my mask with his rostrum, his nose. He swam past me, turned around and came back and bumped my shoulder, then moved directly in front of me and came to a complete stop. I saw that he had fishing line wrapped around his fluke, which was cutting deeply into his skin.

I felt that this little guy was not going to make it! I swam to his side and asked permission to place my hand under his heart. The moment I asked, he fell directly into my arms. It was as if I was holding a human baby. His heart was beating was so fast and he was so scared.

I began transmitting healing energy to the baby, and at the same time another facilitator attempted to undo the fishing line. Unfortunately the line was embedded so deeply that it would have to be cut away from his tail. We called out for someone to bring us a knife.

I asked the facilitator to take care of my snorkeling companion, and before I knew it I was swimming with the baby dolphin in my arms, listening to my internal guidance. I swam with him not knowing where we were heading. After a while his heartbeat returned to normal and he started wiggling in my arms. I asked him if he wanted to go, giving him the choice, hoping he would stay in my arms until we could get some help to cut the line.

I saw his mom coming over to us and I knew he wanted to go to her. I released the baby and he swam to her. Then, to my surprise, three adult dolphins spiraled out of the water all around me, landing right next to me. It was amazing! They knew I had assisted the baby and was helping him to swim. They were saying thank you!

I had never intentionally touched a dolphin. We ask swimmers to refrain from touching them out of respect. As it is, dolphins swim so close to me that we are practically skin-to-skin; we swim heart-to-heart, intimately sharing our time in the water. Our vibrations blend in a soul-to-soul connection, a much higher frequency experience.

You can imagine how profoundly honored I felt when the injured baby trusted me to hold him gently in my arms. As I embraced this beloved baby dolphin, I named him Trusty, for his complete faith in coming to me for help. It was a Divine moment for both of us. We received a healing and a multitude of blessings as the Golden Master Dolphin of Love and Light flowed through my body to this precious one!

I returned to my snorkeling companion, whose life had been changed after witnessing this unusual experience. We swam back to the same area where I first encountered the baby and I was surprised to see the entire pod coming towards me with mom and baby! They swam so close, very slowly approaching my friend, showing us that the baby was OK. Oh, I was so happy! I called to the snorkeler who had gotten a knife to let him know the pod was nearby. He swam over and was able to cut and remove a portion of line that was dragging, thank goodness. I just prayed that this little one would survive when the pod went out to feed for the night.

Back on shore, I started to cry and cry. I felt like I finally gave back to the dolphins after their giving so much to me for all these years! The word got out quickly in our dolphin community: carry a knife!

My friend Lisa was on a boat a few days later and saw the baby. She was able to cut more line off of his fluke. I cried again with joy and relief, so very happy to know that he had lived and was still doing well!

The most wonderful part of this story is that Trusty would come to find me at any of the bays I might be swimming in. We would say hi to each other, feeling so grateful to find one another and sharing our essence, remembering that most incredible, amazing, heart-to-heart experience... with my hand literally placed on his little heart! Today we still communicate with each other; I send him pictures and thoughts of that special day we shared, he receives them and sends his images and feelings back to me. It's like sharing with my most precious best friend, my beloved dolphin I named Trusty. Thank you Trusty, for trusting in me.

Dolphins of 11-11-10

We had somewhere possibly around 400+ dolphins! When we first got in, it was an endless stream of dolphins passing by us. Even after we thought they had all gone by and we were on the boat, I was amazed as I looked again and saw more pods of dolphins heading down to their favorite bay. We got in again, and to my amazement we were surrounded many times over by so many dolphins talking and blowing more bubbles then I have ever seen before.

If you can imagine 200–300 dolphins in the bay, and so many blowing bubbles, all that I could see were tiny bubbles. We also had so many newborn and juveniles leaping and jumping. Without a doubt, we were experiencing the "Light" codes that they were transmitting once more into the waters, just as we were experiencing these "Light" codes ourselves. My friend and I commented how silky the waters felt. Everything was very serene and felt different.

I remember on 11-10-10 the whales held the matrix for the "Light" codes to enter and the dolphins brought these spiraling codes through the waters. That day brought the most "Light Quotient" frequencies ever. The dolphins were telling and showing everyone what we had done together, dolphins and humans working together!

Everyone received the "icosahedrons"—20 crystalline equal triangular faces for their New Light Body! This is incredible beyond what we can comprehend. I am still floating as I am writing these words only hours after my experience. If you open to the energies, you too will be able to receive what I have experienced today. Enjoy the frequencies of unconditional love, peace, harmony, joy and enlightenment that are available if you so choose.

Soon I had the opportunity to experience the Elder pod of dolphins in the bay. A pod came quickly towards me, so excited, triggering my excitement as they headed towards me, sandwiching me on both sides. The energies of this group felt so familiar, it wasn't until they dove under me that I noticed my friend, who I call Tar, was in the group. I hadn't seen Tar in a very long time and here he was with his family. We recognized each other immediately and it was like a greeting of two old close friends. He was introducing me to his family and was very proud of them and himself.

Five years before, I had started swimming with Tar and his mother when he was just a baby. When he became a juvenile we started playing the leaf game. I would take out a leaf, dive down and drop it, then he would dive down and I would retrieve it, repeating this play over and over. He would come up for a breath and dive down and flip it off his tail, flipper or rostrum for me to get. This would go on for as long as one would continue to play. He was really my dolphin playmate until he found his mate and started a family of his own.

To see Tar and his family today brought me so much joy. Instead of just him playing with me, it ended up that his whole family played with me! I feel so grateful to be able to swim with our dolphins and especially my dolphin friends from way back.

Baby Dolphin Passing

In 2012, I was swimming out in the bay when I looked down and saw a baby dolphin in the shallows lying on the bottom of the sand. Its mother was down trying to push the baby as if to wake it up. It was a sad moment. I could tell it had already died. It felt like it just happened, judging by the mother's frantic attempts to help it swim. She would come up for her breath and swim around me a few times, as if to say "Please help my baby."

I believe because of "Pod-Mind," the dolphins that swim in the bay have the memory of all that happens in the bay. This was the same place that the baby dolphin Trusty had come to me for help and survived.

I felt this mom knew who I was and was hoping I could do something. I felt so bad as I communicated to her that I wasn't able to help her baby. I wish I could have been of assistance as she was grieving and it was very sad. I know it is part of life in the water, as we have similar births and deaths as they do. The dolphins are so human-like to me: inspiring, evolved meditation partners, companions and playmates with our leaves…they truly are my best friends!

I stayed with mom for a while longer and then went on to swim with the rest of the dolphins, who were leaving her to be by herself so she could grieve. When I came back, she was still swimming above in circles, no longer diving down to be with her beloved child. It felt like she was saying her goodbyes. She came over a few more times and circled me and I sent her my deepest sympathy and let her know how much I loved her and would be with her while I was on land. This is the connection I have with our dolphins here, resulting from near-daily swims for the last 17 years since 1989! We know each other so well and I am so blessed!

Dolphin Activates Third Eye
May 23, 2011

I was at one of my favorite places to swim with the dolphins from the boat. It is shallow with beautiful turquoise waters. When I first got in I was happily greeted by a group of dolphins. They headed right towards me as I dove down and dropped leaves that I had gathered for our boat trip. We bring them into the bays before we enter the waters; the dolphins love to play the leaf game with us.

They dove down and picked up the leaves, then played for a short time. One dolphin came under me, blowing small bubbles, the one I call Singer. He surfaced next to me, swimming eye-to-eye; and began to circle around and around, having me make these tiny circles only inches from my body, still eye-to-eye. We were so close I wasn't even able to kick.

He was spinning around me, thus having me spin quickly to continue eye contact. There were only inches between us. He was really working with me. I am sure he was activating my third eye. He left with his group of five or six dolphins, as more groups swam under and beside me very actively, loving the leaves I was sharing with them. We must have had over 120 or so dolphins swimming nearby.

Singer, the bubble-blowing dolphin that made sounds as he blew bubbles, once again greeted me. This time he was coming in a direct line; then he circled and then dove under me with his white belly up. They do this as an acknowledgment that they trust us, yet he was doing more. It felt like he was treating me like one of his own and was in a mating vibration and position. The dolphins are always very sensual with each other. They love touching each other, usually flipper-to-flipper; this brings them pleasure and happiness. When they go into mating position one is belly-up. This is what my frisky friend was doing, this being the second time he came and found me very exciting to be around.

To my surprise he came up in front of me with his rostrum (nose) and sent a sonar sound that was very loud only a foot or so from my face, sonaring right into my third eye! Once wasn't enough—he did this three times at close range; I could feel it and hear it at the same time. I stopped and sent him the message, "Why did you sonar me three times?" Whenever anything like this happens in three's, I always take note. To me, anything that happens three times tells me to be aware of what is going on. This message I had learned from my spiritual teacher Dennis Adams as well as Grandma Chandra, who would say the same thing. The number 3 in addition to 13 and 33 are my special spiritual numbers that I have acknowledged as very important all my life.

After getting back on the boat and heading to the harbor, I shared this story with my group. My friends said they could tell the dolphin had sonared me, and I felt altered while doing errands in town later that day. I came home and was ready for a nap—I was wiped out! I walked my dogs and then I was done for the day. Since I had swum so long playing with them, my body felt tired and a little sore, plus the energy from the sonar. I decided to take an Epsom salt bath to relax my muscles. When I was in my bath I went back into the experiences I'd had that day, and my beloved dolphin's energies were with me again. I felt so much love as my body became like a dolphin merging with Singer—I felt a sense of total bliss.

I also had a slight headache at the same time. I believe it was because he had activated my third eye, at the same time bringing my body into bliss. I realized that all my soreness and pain was gone! I believe the bath and allowing the energy to flow through me was his way of saying, "Enjoy your opening into a new level of awareness." This was really incredible. The headache went away as soon as I understood what had happened. I knew I had to write what had taken place immediately to remember it clearly, even though I was still spacey. This was a very important message for me and others, letting people know what the dolphins can do to assist us in our evolution. I have been told that the dolphins are the closest to God, the Divine, Source, All That Is, whatever you might call the Prime Creator.

The whales are the masters of the codes of light, the creation formulas. The whales and dolphins are the species that are able to bring fractal lines, microcosmic and quantum energy planes into harmonics. They project them to you, their whale family. This is the time when the partnership between humans and whales is absolutely key. The dolphins create, because they are part of the creation codes, the whales sing of the harmonics of creation, and the dolphin minds are able to project the fractal line formulas to you. It's all about Love.

Swimming with Whales

The whales

We were so blessed to have the North Pacific humpback whales come each year to the Big Island and other islands to mate and give birth to their calves. The only problem is it is illegal for us to swim with the humpback whales here. After observing these beloved whales for years, I knew it was time to get into the waters so that I could be with them, sharing their space together, having them invite me into their environment, to learn more about these mystical, amazing animals of the sea.

My first time in the water with them was in the Dominican Republic in 2000. In the following years I decided to facilitate my own whale trips and took people to Tonga, which was closer for me, living in Hawaii. My first year taking groups to Tonga was in 2005. I have been taking groups each year up until 2012. I took a break in 2013, feeling I needed to relax. It takes a lot of time and energy to put a trip together for Tonga. In a third-world country where anything can change at any moment, they make the decisions, even whether the airline in Tonga can fly or not fly. This happened once with my group; thus, I know you have to have a lot of patience and perseverance when in a third-world country.

Even with all that, I loved sharing the whales with people, seeing how their lives would change right in front of my eyes! All the time and energy it took to put the trips together was well worth every minute once you get there and have these amazing, life-altering experiences with the beloved whales. The years 2010, 2011 and 2012 were over-the-top, wonderful and intense experiences.

In 2012 they became more present with us, transmitting more healing and life-altering information into the core of our beings, into our cells. Water is a super-conductor of information and the transmissions from the whales were incredible.

I am sharing with you a few of my most memorable trips to the Dominican Republic and Tonga, although I have to say each and every trip to spend time with the whales is unforgettable beyond words.

Swimming with dolphins is like swimming with your best friend; one you love, trust and can really play with and have such joy and fun together. Swimming with the whales is like swimming with the most loving, nurturing, expanded presence of Grace. My first encounter with a humpback whale was very different from the dolphins. It seemed like I was swimming with the Higher Self of the dolphin. They are what I call "Gentle Giants"!

The first time I ever saw a humpback whale in our Hawaiian waters I thought, "Oh my Goddess, it's so big!" Since it is illegal to swim with them here in Hawaii, I was swimming with dolphins when a juvenile whale came from nowhere and swam under me! I stayed still, realizing he was checking me out and at the same time he was transmitting this most unbelievable radiance of light, love and expansiveness. I will never forget that moment of surprise and delight to experience both dolphin and whale energy at the same time.

My next step was to actually go to the place that I could swim with the whales. My friend Joan Ocean was taking a group to the Dominican Republic. I was on to my next adventure, my first whale seminar. This was in February 2000. It was a wonderful trip and at times they were only a few feet from us. We lived on a boat for seven days and became a special family. These experiences expanded and changed my life once again.

Most memorably, one day a mom and calf were swimming directly below me. She began to lift her pec fin up as she began to ascend, then quickly turned and looked me right in the eye! She realized that I was only a few feet above her when she gently pulled her pec fin back to her side. She caught my eye again and surfaced next to me with her baby. She paused for a few minutes before she and her baby glided off. I was so expanded and filled with Love, I didn't function well the rest of the day.

After dinner, although I was so tired, I couldn't sleep and began to journal. It was like automatic writing, it was so fast and so many pages.

This is channeled directly from the mother whale. The mother said, "MOVE INTO THE GREATER REALITY OF ALL THAT IS, ALL THERE HAS EVER BEEN OR WILL EVER BE. WE ARE BEINGS OF LIGHT, WHAT YOU ARE BECOMING AND HAVE ALWAYS BEEN, LIGHT WITHIN LIGHT, LIVING WITHIN THE LIGHT OF YOUR TRUE ESSENCE, ONENESS WITH ONENESS! ALL ENCOMPASSING THE EVERLASTING GLOW OF THE DIVINE. WE ARE ONE!

When I returned home, my 33-year marriage ended; our vibrations no longer supported each other in a healthy way, for I had expanded beyond that which no longer served him or myself.

My second experience was once again to the Dominican Republic. Again, we had amazing encounters and each day was more special then the day before. This trip seemed to be more of a Goddess Adventure, for all were women, excepting two men. This trip turned out to be very sacred with rituals that were never planned, they just happened.

The captain told us that in his 10 years in the DR, he felt this was one of the best and most frequent whale encounters. I believe the special group of women aboard helped create a sacred space with the whales. One woman was pregnant and another desired to become a mother. We did sacred ceremony with the mother and calf whales. This is also a place where mother whales give birth to their young. Right after our ceremony from our small boat, we had an amazing and nurturing close encounter with a Mom and Babe! They knew and felt what we were doing and celebrated when we entered the water. It was a time of Light Expansion and Healing.

Whales of Tonga 2005
My First Trip

Our journey to Tonga started with seven of us leaving Kona for Honolulu, where we picked up our eighth person. We chose the "Luminous Vavaʻu Vessels" as our group name and traveled

together, becoming a pod even before we arrived on the island of Vavaʻu. This was a real blessing as we began a special bond, creating a beautiful human whale pod.

Our trip together was all about "birthing our beingness into new, uncharted territory." Our blessings began with Alessandra's Birthday. This started our "birthing into our essence, into love, light and expansion." Alessandra's birthday fell exactly on our first day on the island and my birthday marked our last day of our stay, representing our physical completion with those amazing, beautiful beings. They assisted us in becoming "who we were always meant to be," allowing us to release all that was no longer serving us and move into our higher reality. This was really only the beginning of our new lives that were to open even further for us all.

Once this process began we became more bonded in an unconditional loving, joyous, heart-centered space with each other. We shared and became the vibration of grace that the whales were transferring to us every moment, whether we were on land or in the water. Their essence was with us continually, as they would swim near and around our island home.

We were like the innocent child with new feelings of excitement, our eyes wide open in wonderment and love with the newness of each moment. We laughed and released old patterns, cried out of joy of what our hearts and eyes beheld.

Our first contact with the magnificent humpbacks of Tonga was with two large whales we named "The Lovers," because of their deep affection for one other. My first words were, "They look like 'my' whales!" Our guide and the owner of the resort said they had never seen these particular whales before, and that they looked like North Pacific humpback whales that migrate to Hawaii to mate and give birth. A little shiver went up my spine, as this was truly what I had also thought. However, since we hadn't seen the South Pacific whales yet, I just shrugged it off.

"The Lovers" were a darker color with no white on their stomachs, which is an identifying feature of the South Pacific whales. It is my belief that somehow this beautiful Hawaiian whale couple had made their way down to Tonga to see us. And I have DVD footage to prove it!

How they got there no one knows. Maybe they were transported by an ET ship? Did these two giant manifestations of highly advanced beings travel beyond space and time right in front of our eyes? We were in awe, having been allowed to witness this miracle, to have enjoyed watching their amazing dance performance as they entwined and spiraled together, holding their pectoral fins in a loving, nurturing embrace as you see in paintings. They flowed together to form a dynamic double helix formation over and over again.

Before we arrived in Tonga, the whales told me that they were going to activate our DNA and RNA. I believe this is what they were symbolizing as they danced and spiraled to the surface to meet our glances of amazement... eye-to-eye, human and whale, spirit-to-spirit, reminding us of our true beingness.

At one point, while watching a whale in front of me, I suddenly felt an immense energy resonating from below me. I looked down to see the other whale's rostrum, its nose, heading straight towards my mask! All I could do was float motionless in the water above him. Just before the whale surfaced, he moved subtly to the side so he would not hurt me with his tail. It was unbelievable that he was able to surface from right below and yet miss me!

This was not the first time I've had whales swim so close when surfacing, yet they never touch me. They are like the dolphins: they know exactly where they are at all times and will never hit or hurt us. The last thing they want is to scare us; they trust us completely with an open heart. They have proven this time and time again. I know we never have to be afraid of these giant yet gentle beings. They are pure loving and nurturing vessels, who are here to teach us to become as they are by constantly modeling behavior to us. What a blessing to have "my" humpback whales come to visit us. Interestingly, they hadn't been seen before or since. This gives us a lot to think about!

Later in the trip we spent three and a half hours with a blessed mother and baby. During one precious moment, the baby dove to mom and she put out her pectoral fins as a mother would do to accept a baby into her arms. It was so nurturing and serene to behold this loving embrace. As the baby became more familiar with us she began to play and interact with us. Meanwhile mom just rested peacefully below, totally trusting us to babysit her calf.

My friend Karen tried an experiment with the mother. She put her arms in front of her, then to the side, three or four times. We watched as the mother copied her movements. I was thinking, "Oh, the movement Karen is making is so wonderful," while at the same time the mother was moving loving energies towards us with her pec fins. She nurtured our souls, as a new mother would do to her baby. We were like her babies too, absorbing her love and nurturance for three and a half hours! We were all positively impacted and shifted at the cellular level by this exchange of maternal love.

Whales of Tonga 2010

I decided to take a Goddess Group to the Ha'apai Islands in Tonga for two weeks. A friend had purchased property there and we stayed at her newly created eco-resort. Unfortunately the weather conditions were challenging for us goddesses! My captain said he was going to cancel our outings for three days in anticipation of the bad weather and that he would make up for the lost days after the storm.

That night after dinner, I conducted a ceremony to activate our "Light Bodies." A very, very large mother whale energy came into the meditation, and I thought, "This is a really large mother!" She seemed so real, yet she was very different: she was in her "Light Body," which explains why she was so big!

The next morning was sunny and beautiful and we wondered if perhaps it was the calm before the storm. After eating breakfast, we asked a Ha'apai fisherman named Cecie if he would take us out to look for whales. He agreed but cautioned us to keep watch for the high winds that were headed our way. We packed a lunch and set off on our adventure in his tiny wooden boat that barely held the eight of us. It was actually quite fun to be only a few feet from the water as we traveled around the islands. Cecie said he knew of a place where the whales "hung out" in a lagoon. We headed that way and saw a few whales here and there, but we wanted to get to the lagoon, knowing that our time on the water was limited.

We had almost reached the lagoon when the winds began to kick up. Cecie suggested that we turn back, as it would take awhile to get back to our island if we were going against the wind and waves. We would be a tiny floating vessel being tossed around on a great big ocean! We all agreed to head back, feeling a little disappointed that we would not meet the whales in the lagoon.

We could see our island in the distance, but in the opposite direction a whale suddenly began to breach repeatedly. We had to quickly decide what we wanted to do. Return to our island or head for the whale? We unanimously voted to go to the whale. So we quickly motored towards the whale as she was still breaching. It was so exciting! We stopped our boat at a safe distance, though we were still very, very close. As she continued to breach, the pounding of her tail on the water was so loud and hard it shook our bodies. Remember, we were in a very small boat and were close to the whale; so having her perform for us was incredible. The way she would slap her tail made me wonder if she was giving birth, and, just as I had this thought, her baby surfaced, and she was not a newborn! Momma began to tail-slap, and the baby started breaching over and over again.

This was truly the largest mother (of any whale!) I had ever seen in all my years swimming with the whales. She was enormous! She moved a second time with her baby, and a male escort surfaced next to her, blowing his long-held breath. We were with a mom, baby and escort! We followed them for a short distance and watched as they dove and disappeared. Cecie stopped the boat, and I told my friends to BE READY. I wasn't sure why, but I knew if we were going to get in with them it would be quick.

My friend Susan, who is a whale sister, and I were hanging with our feet in the water, barely holding on, when the mother appeared to lunge towards our boat. She was not in direct alignment with the boat but she was heading our way. When I saw her back cresting out of the water I though "Oh, my Goddess, she is really, really huge!" The next thing I knew, she had pulled me into the water, as though she were a giant magnet! In I went, with Susan right behind me. As for the rest of my story, everything that occurred from this point forward happened within a matter of seconds.

My arm went up to show whomever had a chance to get in the water that I saw the whale. She was a little to the right, maybe 15 feet or so underneath us with her baby slip-streaming on top of her back. My hand was still in the air as she sped towards me, looking me right in the eye.

For a frozen moment, we were eye-to-eye, just a few feet apart. As she was passing, her eye moved rapidly, as if gyrating. She opened her eye so wide that I could see the sclera (white part) of her eye all around the iris (pigmented portion). I didn't know that whales could do this!

Through her rapid eye movements I sensed that she was quickly and deliberately transferring Soul Information to me, third eye to third eye. She then turned her enormous body towards me so that we were heart-to-heart, as her throat pleats bellowed in and out. I had one panicked thought as this was happening so quickly: "Where is her tail?" She was so close that I was momentarily concerned her giant tail would swat me! Suddenly there were bubbles all around me, and I looked just ahead to see her tail ten feet in front of me. With a small flick of her fluke, she and her baby were gone! We never saw them again. Afterwards, we all wondered how she swam to me so fast without hitting me.

 I then realized that this was the whale that was in our meditation the previous night. We were meant to communicate with her, and she called us in. It was no wonder we made the choice to go to her instead of heading back to our island. We made it safely back; it was as if she had calmed the waters for our return. Wow, what an experience!

The interesting part was that after this exchange I became so sick I could hardly make it to my *fale*, where we sleep. For three days, I was unable to get out of bed except to use the bathroom, and I survived on a diet of coconut water. My illness coincided with the three-day cancellation of our boat outings. On the fourth day, when the boat picked us up, I felt great... like nothing had happened! What a big shift!

Indeed, a lot did happen. I learned from my inner guidance. This mother whale and I had an agreement to meet and exchange our frequencies, eye-to-eye, heart-to-heart! She gave me the patterns of her whale essence, as I gave her my human/spirit essence patterns. It was a complete and equal exchange. My life from that day forward shifted dramatically in every way, as did the lives of the other Goddess participants.

Tonga Humpback Whales 2011
"Portal of Light"

Whale's eye

My two-week trip to swim with the South Pacific Humpback Whales in September 2011 was one of the most fantastic, incredible, amazing experiences! I knew that my trip in 2011 was going to be life-altering and elevate us to a higher frequency at the cellular level of our Being. I usually have eight or nine people on my trips per week, yet people were coming from all over. They too sensed a Big Shift was to happen with the assistance of the whales for the 144,000 crystalline grids of our beloved Mother Earth.

Those who gathered created a "Portal of Light and Love" in the waters of Tonga. I had 12 people on the first week and 13 on the second week. It was the largest group ever, yet at the same time all of us became a wonderful Spiritual Family and most of us are still in contact and see each other. The whales said it took this many people to create this "Portal" so we could shift the planet and ourselves into a higher frequency that was needed to assist the larger and important energy shifts of 2012!

Every day spent with the whales was beyond words and so special for each of us. I had one beautiful participant, Candy, who was such an Angel! She brought a Lemurian crystal necklace for each person as well as a T-shirt that said "Sistars" on it. Aurora, a very good friend of Candy's, works traveling all over the world putting crystals at places that need light, to shift stagnate energies. Aurora channels the "Beings Beyond the Realm," a very special group of ETs. After hearing me say that the three of us were Sistars, Candy got the idea to put "Sistars" on the shirts.

Candy had sent my Lemurian crystal months before. She had the crystal activated by "Little Grandma," an amazing young shaman woman. Shortly before my whale trip to Tonga, I was in

Mt. Shasta at Trish and Doug's seminar. We had a private session with Susan, who owned the Shambhala Center, with the 13th crystal skull. The 13th crystal skull had the ability to activate other crystal skulls. I had my Lemurian crystal necklace activated and took it to Tonga to have the whales activate it more. I took it swimming with me almost daily. Having a fully charged crystal from Little Grandma, dolphins, and the 13th crystal skull, now it was the whales' turn. We had a ceremony where each participant was able to hold my crystal with their crystal necklace, so they could receive all that these crystals held within them. We were united and reunited from the first day!

The seminar started on September 13th, the next day being my birthday, as I have spent my birthday with the whales for eight years. To my horror, a miscommunication had happened: a small boat in poor condition showed up that would only take six people and I had twelve people standing with me wanting to get on the boat! Where was my boat and my special captain, John, I had each year?

We had a new owner of the resort standing next to me. He said, "Wait one moment," and made a call, saying that all would be OK, he had a boat on its way! It all happened so fast! In fifteen minutes a big, beautiful boat was heading our way. I must have had a look of shock on my face, for Shane, the owner, said, "Yes this is your boat, Happy Birthday!" What a surprising and wonderful birthday present. It was the most incredible day with the whales and my friends who became my Lemurian family!

Shane gave us this beautiful boat for the rest of the two weeks at the price I was paying for a smaller boat. How does it get any better than this? We were so looked after by the whales as well as so many other Beings of Light! This boat had two cabins with showers in each cabin, a full-size kitchen, an upper deck, and a huge deck in front and back that had an outdoor shower. Additionally there was a platform to easily slide off from to swim with the whales! We had this boat up until the time one of the engines needed some repair, so Shane gave us one of his other boats that, believe it or not, was even bigger! It had four separate cabins below instead of two cabins. What a way to start my birthday and our incredible, evolving two weeks with the beloved whales!

This was going to be the activation day as we headed out to be with the whales, a very big day for each of us as well as humanity!

We entered an area in the channel that was very close to 19.5 degrees latitude. We felt a very special frequency when we were be in this area, not realizing this until we were shown on a map that it was around 19.5. I live on the Big Island, which is also at 19.5 degrees latitude. For me this energy was very familiar. Aurora said this was the spot to do our blessings for the waters with the crystals she and Candy had brought, as well as the place that the Lemurian crystalline whale codes were to be transmitted to everyone.

I asked that we all gather in the back of the boat. It was time for the Whale Codes to be given to each person. It was as if my body went through the entire activation that the mother whale in Kona had transmitted to me in March. I felt the same frequencies enter my body, the sounds of the "Crystalline" permeated every cell of my body as they were being transferred to each person. These crystalline whale codes were given to each participant with the highest blessings from the whales that encircle our beloved Mother Earth. Gaia, the soul of our earth, flowed up into each person as the Sirian energies from my Star Ship of One, above us, flowed down to each individual.

It is very powerful to receive these codes; they are only transferred by permission from the Council of One, my Sirian Star Ship. These Lemurian crystalline codes are also only transferred to others when permission is given. They are for those who are receiving them to be used for their higher evolution and not for them to transfer to others. This was made very clear to me when I had transferred codes on my 2012 whale trip and forgot to mention that this is for them only, not transferable. If one tried to give these Codes to another it wouldn't happen; the Codes were transmitting within my Soul. They are Lemurian Codes of the fifth dimension. So sweet was this day of fifth-dimensional balance and harmony for Humanity!

What great service my whale podners gave to themselves and all upon beloved Mother Earth! I am so grateful to my 2011 Sis-Stars and Bro-Stars for their commitment!

We had so many incredible days with the whales. On our last day out we had the pleasure of spending nearly five hours with a two-year-old singer. He would hang below us singing his heart out to us! In only a few minutes, your DNA changes when a male whale sings to you. Can you imagine having a sweet young male under us for that long? When a whale is directly under you, your entire body vibrates, every cell in your body vibrates, and it is very, very loud! This juvenile was sending the New Crystalline Whale codes around the world through the waters, our bodies, at a cellular level, becoming the song!

What a gift he gave us on our last day. On our way home we were all laying flat out on the deck, it was as if we couldn't move from all the whale song. Our captain yelled out that there was a mom and baby calf close to the shore in the shallows. I heard him say it, yet my body could hardly move to take a look. Others were trying to put on their gear to go, but it was so funny to watch us in slow motion. It seemed like an incredible task to put on our fins! This is what the song had done to us; we were like rag dolls attempting to move! It would have been great if someone had filmed us getting ready to greet the mom and baby. I was so glad we did go and say hi to them. The mom was sleeping and the baby would gently come join us. It was also as if the calf was moving in slow motion to match our state of bliss! I believe as we joined this mom and her newborn baby in the shallows, our encounter symbolized the birthing of the song of the crystalline codes within us. This was one of the happiest last days ever!

Now you would think, "How could it get any better than this?", when it did. We were almost to our resort when we looked down and there was a pod of spinner dolphins escorting us back. We docked and they kept going on down the channel as if to say "good-bye" to our group and thanking us along with the whales for our service to humanity in creating a "Lemurian Portal" and activating the 144,000 crystalline grids of our beloved Mother Earth, the Soul of Gaia.

Close Encounter
Whale Assistance in Hawaii

I am sharing this beautiful story with you to show you how the whales and the dolphins can assist us in times of challenges. As I have mentioned before it is illegal to swim with the humpback whales in Hawaii where I live. I had an amazing experience one day in a stormy high surf. The dolphins were swimming in the usual area of the bay; a few people were actually in the water with them. I stopped and looked out to see if I could see some whales. I saw a blow quite far out, I felt like this whale was calling to me. I went in at another area away from where the dolphins were to see if I could hear whale song. To my amazement I could hear a whale loudly as I entered the water; you can hear their song from a distance. Since it was so far out I thought I would swim and listen to its song, which was so beautiful. When we are with the whales and dolphins, time seems to shift into another reality or space that is elevated and we lose the experience of "time" as we know it. This was certainly my experience on this special day.

The waves were more like swells, yet I didn't realize where I was swimming or how far out I was, since "time" was shifting by the song of the whale. The whale's song kept moving from one area to another, sometimes very loud, as though it were under me, then it would get fainter, then loud again. It was obviously moving around, the waters were so murky that I couldn't see anything; I could only hear this incredible song that was being sung to me. I believe that he had come under me a few times and that this beloved whale was communicating and sharing its vibrations with me.

At one point I looked up over the waves and realized I was very far out and began to feel cold. When I looked back towards shore I was wondering, "How am I going to swim back in through all these swells, being cold already, knowing I would get colder?" I decided to head back; again I felt the energy of the whale, knowing he was swimming under me as I was heading back to shore. He then began to sing his song again, this time leading me back to shore safely.

Even though I couldn't see this dear whale, he sang me all the way into the shore! I was almost there when he dove under me, only fifteen feet or so below me in the shallow waters. I could see him with his rostrum (nose) pointed down and his fluke (tail) directly under me as he began sounding his song again, letting me know I was OK and had made it back.

I was so cold that I was shaking as well as shaking from the vibration frequencies he was sounding into the earth. I felt this beloved whale was helping to stabilize the waters for it seemed it was getting stormier. Just as I was saying goodbye and thanking him for being there and sharing his message with me, he stopped singing and slowly came straight up towards me, surfaced only three feet from me, blew, dove again, and with a quick tail thrust he was gone.

When I got to the car and saw what time it was I couldn't believe I had been in these crazy waters for three hours with this amazing whale friend. How could I refuse his whale song invitation? How blessed I am.

Messages from the Whales:

HUMANITY IS NOW IN A TIME OF TRANSITION AS MANY OF YOU ALREADY KNOW AND ARE EXPERIENCING. MOST OF OUR BODIES ARE POLLUTED WITH UNNECCESSARY THINGS, TOXINS THAT ARE CAUSING US NOT TO FUNCTION IN A NORMAL WAY. WE SEE THIS UNFORTUNATE OIL SPILL IN THE GULF AS AN OPPORTUNITY FOR ALL BEINGS TO CLEAN UP THEIR OWN BODIES. AS YOU BEGIN TO CLEAR YOUR BODIES, THIS IS A PERFECT WAY TO ASSIST MOTHER EARTH GAIA IN CLEANSING HER OWN BODY. WHENEVER A SITUATION LIKE THE GULF HAPPENS, IT IS FOR A HIGHER REASON. WE SEE THIS AS A MOST IMPORTANT TIME FOR ALL BEINGS LIVING ON PLANET EARTH AND ELSEWHERE TO COME TOGETHER IN UNITY FOR A HIGHER PURPOSE, TO SERVE ALL HUMANITY AND MOTHER EARTH.

WHEN WE SAY CLEANING UP OUR BODIES WE THE WHALES ARE REFERRING TO OUR THOUGHTS AND ACTIONS CONTRIBUTING TO SAVING OUR BELOVED PLANET FROM FURTHER DESTRUCTIVE SITUATIONS. MOTHER EARTH IS IN US AND WE ARE IN MOTHER EARTH! PLEASE, WE ASK YOU TO URGENTLY SEE WE ARE ONE AND THE SAME BEINGS.

WHEN WE SEE THIS AS OUR DEEPEST TRUTH THEN EVERYTHING BEGINS TO FALL INTO PLACE AND OUR BODIES ALONG WITH MOTHER EARTH'S BODY WILL AUTOMATICALLY BEGIN TO HEAL ITSELF!

WE CAN HEAL OURSELVES SIMPLY BY OUR THOUGHTS, FEELINGS, AND ACTIONS THAT WE PRESENT TO SITUATIONS EVERY DAY. EACH AND EVERY MOMENT IS A PRECIOUS MOMENT. WHEN WE SEE THIS IS OUR TRUTH THEN ALL THINGS CLEAR WITHOUT MUCH TO DO. IT IS PART OF THE COSMIC PLAN FOR ALL LIVING BEINGS ON THE EARTH PLANE. WE SWIM AMONGST YOU IN HOPES THAT YOU WILL BEGIN TO SEE US AS 'EMMISSARIES OF LIGHT.' WE CARRY THE SAME LIGHT AS YOU DO. WHEN YOU SEE US, FEEL US, OR HAVE THE CHANCE TO LOOK IN OUR EYES BY

PHOTO OR ACTUAL ENCOUNTER, WE ARE BRINGING CONSCIOUS AWARENESS TO EVERYTHING AROUND YOU. IT IS OUR HOPE THAT YOU CAN SEE THE MAGNIFICENCE THAT YOU ARE AND WHY YOU ARE HERE.

ONE REASON YOU ARE HERE IS TO EVOLVE WITH MOTHER EARTH GAIA INTO HIGHER FREQUENCIES OF LOVE AND LIGHT AND BRING THE PEACE WE ARE ALL LOOKING FOR. LET'S COME TOGETHER NOW AND SUPPORT EACH OTHER IN DOING THE BEST WE CAN TO LIVE TOGETHER IN PEACE AND HARMONY. YOU WILL SEE THE GOLDEN AGE THAT YOU ARE LOOKING FOR. IT IS POSSIBLE EVEN WITH THE SITUATIONS AND EARTH CHANGES THAT ARE HAPPENING AT THIS TIME. THESE ARE THE MOST IMPORTANT TIMES TO COME TOGETHER IN UNITY AND BRING ABOUT CHANGE.

BY THE OIL SPILL EXPERIENCE WE NOW HAVE A WINDOW OF OPPORTUNITY TO CLEAR OLD STUFF AS YOU CALL IT FROM YOUR BODIES AND MOVE FREQUENCY TO A MUCH HIGHER LEVEL OF HUMAN AND PLANETARY EXISTENCE. WE SEE THIS AS THE OPPORTUNITY TO WORK WITH THE TWELFTH DIMENSIONAL FREQUENCIES. BY HEALING OTHERS AND OURSELVES IN A PERMANENT AND LASTING WAY WE THE WHALES ARE HERE FOR ALL HUMANITY. PLEASE LOOK TO US AS ASSISTING YOU TO FURTHER BRING PEACE, LOVE, LIGHT, JOY, AND HARMONY UPON OUR BELOVED MOTHER EARTH GAIA AND OURSELVES. WE WHALES ARE CARRYING THE FREQUENCIES OF THE COSMOS. WE ARE HERE FOR YOU. WE LOVE YOU. PLEASE REMEMBER WE ARE YOU AND YOU ARE US!

1-9-11 Whale Communication

Since there weren't dolphins this morning, I went to see what messages I could get from the whales. I took a long walk in the City of Refuge on this most gloriously beautiful day. As I was nearing my favorite lookout spot where you can see for miles, I noticed a couple of whale spouts and activity. Watching them for quite a while, I then began to make my way up to one of my favorite sacred spots.

Butterflies began to fly around me and I had the thought to call in the Lemurian energies to be present. As I looked out, walking along, I saw two whales swimming in the direction I was walking. My heart was so filled with such joy! I yelled out, "I love you, thank you so much for coming with me!"

I stopped and tuned into their frequencies, getting quite a download. It was incredible. Sitting in my sacred place and just looking out in gratitude, I saw that far out a whale was coming towards me. It looked like a young whale. I sat there in my bliss for some time communing with this very special juvenile who made its presence known many times. We were sending our thoughts and feelings to each other consciously—it was wonderful!

Heading to the car, I looked out once more. Again, I saw this juvenile whale swimming along with me as I was walking. He had stayed with me from my sacred spot. I told him, "I would be in the water with you if I could," as we were exchanging energies.

I thought about an experience once before in Del Mar when I first saw the dolphins. The same thing happened as I was walking along the beach: the dolphins followed me just as this whale was doing. That wonderful day was my beginning of communications with the cetaceans. Unless you count my initial communication with whale energy in the story of *Moby Dick*, the book I would hold as a young child before going to sleep. This was my real beginning in communicating with the cetaceans.

As I walked further, I saw my seventh and eighth whales for the day, a mom and calf, which might have been the first ones I saw earlier. They were very close to the shoreline. I could hear their big breath when they came up and traveled. What an end to a most beautiful day!

WHALE MESSAGE:

JANUARY IS A NEW BEGINNING FOR THIS NEW YEAR, TIME FOR PEOPLE TO SLOW DOWN, TO TAKE TIME TO SEE WHAT IS ABOUT YOU IN THE VERY MOMENT...NOT LOOKING TO SEE WHAT IS NEXT. SLOW DOWN AND TAKE TIME. NOW YOU CAN SMELL THE ROSES AND ACTUALLY TAKE A BREATH, GAIN INSIGHT OF THIS MOMENT. BEGIN TO SEE WHAT IT IS YOU ARE LOOKING FOR IN LIFE. MOVING TOO FAST GETS YOU NOWHERE. IF YOU ARE TOO BUSY, YOU LOSE WHAT IS RIGHT IN FRONT OF YOU AND YOU DON'T SEE. PLEASE TAKE THE TIME TO SEE THE REAL YOU AND KNOW THEM WELL. SEE EVERYONE WITH INDIVIDUAL EYES, FEEL THE ENERGY OF LOVE AND JOY AS THEY BEGIN TO TAKE OVER YOUR FIELD OF VISION BEFORE YOU INTO BOTH INNER AND OUTER REALMS.

BE MORE PLAYFUL BY TAKING THE TIME TO PLAY.

BE MORE LOVING BY LOVING YOURSELF AND OTHERS MORE AS THEY ARE INSTEAD OF HOW YOU THINK THEY SHOULD BE OR ACT. BE MORE CONSCIOUS OF WHAT IS AROUND YOU IN EVERY MOMENT. THEN EACH NEXT MOMENT WILL BRING YOU PLEASURE LIKE NEVER BEFORE.

LOVE YOUR ENVIRNOMENT AND IT WILL LOVE YOU BACK BY PROVIDING A STABLE FOUNDATION FOR YOU TO LIVE UPON. LOVE MOTHER EARTH FOR THE GIFT THAT SHE GIVES YOU: YOUR VERY EXPERIENCE OF LIFE UPON HER. SHE WILL GIVE BACK LESS UNPLEASANT MOVEMENTS OF ENERGY AS QUAKES AND STORMS.

LOVE, DIVINITY, SOURCE, GOD...WHATEVER YOU RESONATE WITH, YOUR LIFE WILL BE ONE OF LOVE, PEACE, AND JOY IN EVERY MOMENT.

YOU AND THE DIVINE ARE ONE!

WE THE WHALES HOPE YOU ENJOY THIS NEW YEAR AS MUCH AS WE ENJOY MAKING OUR PRESENCE KNOWN TO YOU FOR ALL TO SEE, HEAR, AND FEEL AS OUR MESSAGES COME THROUGH THIS SOURCE AVAILABLE TO YOU SO THAT YOU TOO CAN FEEL US.

WE LOVE YOU, THE WHALES

One Sunday, bright and beautiful at the end of January, I encountered a humpback whale while in a kayak at Kona Village. I was invited to meet friends at the Kona Village for lunch. I was sharing my upcoming Tonga trip details when I spotted a whale breaching in front of us. Just as I had been sharing my experience with the mother whale in the Kingdom of Tonga when I saw the whale there breaching, so this whale in Hawaii also seemed to be responding in the same way. Did this whale know I was talking about my experience and confirm it by breaching?

We continued to discuss one of the largest mother whales I had ever seen, when more whales began to make themselves known with blows, breaches and playful gestures for us to see beside the hotel. We knew we couldn't take the hotel's kayaks out past the buoys, so we only watched from shore.

Then I see a whale surface inside the buoys! My friend and I took two kayaks sitting at the shoreline and went out. Another man also took one, as he too saw the whale. The two of them went off in a slightly different direction than me, yet my guidance was to keep going in the direction I was heading. We all stopped and waited inside the zone where we could have the kayaks. After a while my ego thought to paddle a little more toward the others but I stopped and said, "I feel you somewhere in here," so I waited.

A few minutes later, I heard the blow of the whale and quickly turned my kayak in that direction. Before I could even put my paddle into the water, it surfaced and headed right at me. It looked me in the eye and dove down under my kayak!

Needless to say, my kayak was caught in the turbulence of the whale's tail. At that time I wasn't sure if my kayak and I were to become whale riders! What fun!

Later, I realized that the first spot had been where the whale was, most likely lying below me, yet my ego got in the way, thinking if the other two people are looking in a different direction I must move towards them. My intuition was right: it taught me to pay closer attention and not be influenced by what other people are doing. Oh, these lessons we are learning! I feel this was getting me ready for my upcoming Tongan whale adventure soon approaching when I can get right into the water without worrying about being caught or fined.

Heart-to-Eye Activation
South Pacific/North Pacific Mother Whales

The eye and heart activation experience in Tonga with the mother whale and my experience months later in the "Birthing of the Golden Lemuria" seminar was a preparation for my vessel (or body) to be able to hold the "New Crystalline Whale Codes." This was so they could be transferred to our beloved Mother Earth, her Soul, to Gaia, through the 144,000 crystalline grids that make up our planet, to assist all humanity in elevating their energy frequency and energy fields into the "light-filled" fifth dimension of Lemuria.

These two amazing mother whales held the same frequency and were making the same gestures in the Tongan South Pacific as in Hawaii's North Pacific. It showed me there is no time or space, it is all an illusion, there is only the "Now" moment. Hopefully, we will all use these precious moments spent in love, light and compassion for each other.

I was given the Soul name of Ke Waine Ka Kalima, the Mother/Protectress of the Sea, by Master Sha and confirmed by a well-known Kahuna. It is my passion to protect the dolphins and whales. In many ways, their importance to our survival is immeasurable. They are here to assist us. Hopefully we will all understand this importance as we learn more about who they are and why they are here.

Beyond the sheer joy of swimming together, we experience a Presence together and we are changed at the core of our being. We will all be learning more as time goes by.

I carry these patterns: the triangle codes from our North Pacific, the South Pacific and the Atlantic humpback whales, plus the codes of 3 and 33, my personal vibrational number fields.

With the eye activation of the mother whale in Tonga, an equal exchange took place from our third eyes. I received her DNA pattern of the humpback whales. She received my pattern of human DNA codes. We had an agreement to exchange these patterns at this exact timing.

This was the preparation for the agreed timing that the North Pacific mother whale and I would come together, so she could transfer the new crystalline whale codes for humanity within my being. This was at a cosmic level: the codes were to be transmitted and grounded into beloved Mother Earth at this exact time. Grandma Chandra knew this was the timing for humanity and the crystalline grids of Gaia to be upgraded with these new crystalline whale codes.

This seemed to be my Mission in this lifetime. What a blessing it is for me to be a Steward between the cetaceans—the dolphins and whales—and humanity.

Chapter 5

Spiritual Awakenings and Inspirational Teachers

Dennis Adams

In 1976 my life underwent a complete change. I started thinking about my OWN HEALING WITHIN MYSELF instead of constantly giving out to others. This led me on my own healing path, which I still follow today, always evolving myself to the next level.

My first physical Master Teacher was a wonderful man named Dennis Adams. He was truly a Master in showing that EVERYTHING IS YOU, NOTHING IS OUTSIDE OF YOURSELF.

This was back in 1976. We were the first group he shared his wisdom with. The most important thing I liked about Dennis was that he didn't call himself a Guru, Psychic, or anything. He was no different from us. WE ARE ALL THE SAME!

Even though he was an alchemist, being documented teaching in two different places, he kept stating the fact that We Are All The Same! This is one of the reasons I studied with him. HE TAUGHT GOD/GODDESS IS WITHIN!! These statements were on T-shirts that he had made up for us.

Scientists under controlled conditions documented that Dennis could change salmonella poison with his mind and focus it into something else under the microscope. He proved the power of our minds.

He also spent eight years in the woods with only small amounts of food brought to him from time to time. An amazing story he told us was he was getting hungry for protein and needed some meat. One day he went searching for food and a deer appeared before him. They acknowledged and communicated with each other; Dennis needed meat for his body. The deer lay down and gave his body to him knowing he was helping Dennis to have the nourishment that he required. This was an act of kindness from the deer. They co-created an amazing experience in sharing soul-to-soul. It was very beautiful how it was described.

Dennis was amazing. In one of our weekend seminars he was speaking to the group when he suddenly appeared as Jesus in full form without stopping what he had been saying to us. He was the image of Jesus as I would have recognized Jesus to look like. I kept looking at him when, as he continued talking, he was once again Dennis! I turned to my friend next to me and we both looked like: "What happened? Did you see Jesus?"

We said nothing until breaktime, when a few others said, "Oh my God, he shape-shifted into Jesus right in front of our eyes without skipping a beat." This was the first time I actually experienced his ability to shape-shift.

Dennis had a weeklong intensive seminar in Mt. Shasta, where he lived. I knew when I signed up it was going to be an intense yet amazing time. A Galactic Convention began with ETs and UFO ships coming in as we were arriving. It felt like we were part of their convention as they were part of our convening together.

Dennis told us this is what is happening and to expect some amazing miracles. It seemed that miracles would be happening within us as we watched what was taking place outside of us.

One of my favorite memories was during the last part of our week. We went out on the property where Dennis was building a home. We were working on a sweat lodge for that evening. Some of us went out looking for firewood, which I did, and some stayed to help Dennis build the sweat lodge. When we came back there was such a commotion around the fire.

Dennis (on purpose) lit the fire with kerosene to make a huge blaze of fire shoot out, catching his arm on fire. A Doubting Thomas grabbed a blanket and tried to put out the fire on his arm. Dennis told him to stand back, and when he did Dennis's arm was OK, with no visible signs that it had caught fire!

As the story was shared, he said the reason he had lit the fire as he did was to prove to the Doubting Thomas that his fear actually created this experience. Dennis did this purposely to show others what our fears can do. The blanket had burn holes in it from the fire, yet Dennis's arm showed no signs of anything ever happening. Yes, there were others that witnessed this event.

It was a neverending adventure when you were with Dennis; not only was he highly intelligent, he was always making you laugh!

I studied with Dennis for six years, then took his work out to apply it to others and myself. This is what he told us would happen. One day it would be "time to leave the nest," as he used to call it. This is exactly what happened in my last seminar in Mt. Shasta with him; interestingly it happened for those of us who had started studying with Dennis at the beginning of his teachings. What a fabulous learning I received from him.

Huna Mystery School

I had been a student of Dennis Adams for about a year when a mysterious flyer ended up in my mailbox. I lived in Cool California, a gated community, so didn't know how or where it came from. I was very curious about this flyer. It was a weekend teaching from the Nevada City mystery school that was to be taught in Sacramento. I lived a half an hour from Sacramento at the time.

The night it began I didn't go, but when I woke up early the next morning I knew I was to be there. I called the number on the flyer and a woman answered saying, "We have your seat saved and we are waiting for you to arrive!"

First of all, how did they know I would be coming or that I would come after missing the first night? It's interesting because this was an intensive class and you usually aren't able to miss the first night.

It would start in the early morning, sometimes going until midnight before it ended. Also, we weren't able to speak about the class with anyone, even when we went to lunch; we all went together in silence.

I had never experienced a teaching like this where the material was kept in secret. These teachings were from the mystery school of Huna and kept only between the initiates.

I was definitely inspired by the Lemurians to get these ancient secret teachings. In the timeline of Lemuria (what we would consider the past of long ago), many teachings were given this way: you had to be invited by an Elder or Dream Keeper who taught us our profession that we would use to help others.

This was really a sacred initiation for me to begin to remember Lemuria and my fifth-dimensional energy. Divine Order was in play and I took the Huna mystery school course in two days!

These are some of the unusual events that came to me out of nowhere. As I began to have more of these types of experiences, I realized the Angels and my Teachers of Light, the Lemurians, created these adventures for me, making an amazing difference in my life.

Trance Channeler: Jabar and Lauren

During this same year, 1977, while still living in Cool, my friend and I drove to Shingletown to a bookstore for the fun of it. While we were there a man came down the aisle towards me and gave me a hug. This was not just a hug; this hug held energies that were so powerful and amazing we continue hugging for it seemed like forever.

When we looked into each other's eyes, I knew him and he knew me even though we had never physically met. He mentioned he was going to give a free talk that evening regarding crystal healing of the body. This sounded interesting and I felt excited to go. He said he would be teaching a crystal-healing workshop in Sacramento over the weekend. I told him I would like to come back that evening, although I wouldn't be able to come to the workshop because my husband and I would be going up to Chico to help my daughter move.

After he walked away, two of his bodyguards came up to me saying they were very surprised he hugged me, as he had just done a channeling for the owner and after he channels no one is to touch him.

This explained why the hug was so overwhelming to me. They also said they knew me, that I was part of the Orion soul group that they and Lauren came from.

The evening talk was amazing. Lauren, who is a trance channeler (the first I ever met), went out of this body and the entity "Jabar" merged into his.

In the past, Lauren played professional football for the San Francisco 49ers. He was truly a big guy! But when "Jabar," a very old entity, was present, his body became a very short, bent-over old man!

This happened right in front of my eyes. This was the second time I watched someone change their body from one form or presence to any other. Dennis Adams could also shape-shift into others at will.

Lauren asked if I was coming to the workshop in the morning and even though I loved the channeling, I had to say no, I wouldn't be able to join the class. I went home that evening and went out onto my balcony and looked up at the stars, and to my amazement there were the three stars of the Orion belt.

The next morning I woke up and told my husband about the evening and how I would love to go to the workshop for advancing my healing abilities, and to my surprise (or shock) he encouraged me go. He said that he would go help my daughter and that he knew I was to go!

My husband mostly rejected things like this and here he was saying, yes go! He wasn't even upset. He was happy for me to be able to go. This showed me how the higher forces come through for us.

I quickly got ready and drove to Sacramento, to my next beautiful adventure. When I arrived at the hotel, only a few people were there and I was nearly late. I knew more people had signed up for I had seen them do so at the evening event, so where were they?

Lauren saw me, not surprised at all, and motioned for me to sit in a certain chair in the front. I greeted him and sat down. After a few minutes the bodyguards closed the doors and as I looked around there were only seven of us, all sitting in the front row. Lauren said "Jabar" told him to shut the doors and that they were to begin the class. Why only seven, I wondered?

Lauren then said "Jabar" had told him there were really only seven of us who were supposed to be there and that all the rest of the people who signed up either got lost in finding the place or something happened at the last minute.

Again this was confirmation that we are always in the right place at the right time! This was one of Dennis Adams' wonderful teachings.

Lauren then said he was going to go out and watch a movie while "Jabar" would be using his body. In a few minutes I once again witnessed this remarkable shifting of Lauren's body into Jabar, the old ancient man.

Jabar began to speak to us in a very different voice and said he was going to tell each of us who we are, what we were doing and will be doing in the future. I have had readings before, yet this seemed different.

He told us that we were all emotional body healers; although there was one among us that was a little different in the way she would heal others. He then came over to me and put his hands on my head and told me this was how I would heal others. I could use the crystal-healing technique as a tool, yet at some point this is how I would be healing others, like Jesus did.

My first thought was, "Oh gee, here we go again, making me different from the others and possibly having them be jealous." It wouldn't be the first time, even though I didn't feel they had reason to be jealous of me. I only held them in my heart.

There wasn't time to feel it out anyway because Jabar started pairing people up to work on each other. As they moved to do the healing work on each other I was sitting in the chair by myself thinking, "What am I supposed to do now?"

Jabar gave instructions as to what they were to do, and then he said to me that he was going to leave the body and have Lauren come back, once Lauren was lying on the floor. I was to go over to Lauren and do a healing on him. I was to only touch his head and I would know what to do, I would be guided.

Again, I was asking myself what am I going to do, then the next moment the thought was gone and I was sitting at the head of Lauren. Just as I was about to put my hands on his head, his assistant came over and tried to tell me not to touch him when he is in a trance.

Jabar said it was OK. I was to heal Lauren. I found out later no one had ever been allowed to do a healing on Lauren. It continued to get more and more interesting. I put my hands on his head and could feel the healing energies being transmitted to him.

After a while Lauren opened his eyes, looking surprised to see where he was and not at the movie any longer. He quickly closed his eyes for some time, then he opened them again and said the healing was complete. He asked me to follow him outside. He wanted to talk to me.

He then told me about our connection to Orion and past connections. We both wondered some days later if we had come into this life to share it together, but when Lauren asked Jabar he said not now. I had a certain mission to fulfill as he had his own and we both needed to complete what we came here to do. I knew we had a certain love and will always share that whether we ever saw each other or not again. I was married at the time and wanted to be with my husband.

Ascension Teacher Joanna Cherry

I started working with an Ascension teacher named Mark Schuff. I loved the classes he would hold. It was as if I was reacquainting my body with my light body once more. I had never really forgotten; I was re-awoken. Mark's teacher Joanna Cherry was giving an "Ascension" class in Mt. Shasta. I was living in Redding at the time and drove up with a couple of my friends.

One night after the class we drove up to the Mountain. It was so cold, snow was everywhere. We stopped and walked not far from the car when I suddenly smelled a sweet fragrance all around me.

I couldn't figure out what it was and why was it around me on this cold night; how could I smell anything? I asked the other girl who was with me if she smelled a fragrance that was strong, yet very calming? She didn't. We quickly went back to the car to keep from freezing. When we closed the doors I asked if any of the other girls had noticed a fragrance. They also said no, but then the next moment the fragrance was in the car! What was this?

One of my friends channeled the Ashtar Command and she said they were telling her that we needed to get back to the house, they wanted to talk with us. We drove back, got our chairs in a circle ready for them to show up. It was a quiet night with no wind. We were staying at a home that was surrounded by trees.

She began to open her channel to the Ashtars when the wind began to pick up and became a force. It got really loud, blowing the trees back and forth. The Ashtar Command said they were above us in their ship, this was why the wind and the sound.

They told each of us something about ourselves that was right-on, plus what they saw for each of us. It was so lovely, the feelings I had and the serenity that I felt as they were transmitting information to us. We asked what the fragrance was we smelled; they said it wasn't from this dimension, it was from where they lived, explaining that it was close to what we would call "frankincense and myrrh."

When I think about it, it truly was that smell, only more beautiful and heavenly. What a wonderful gift we received that special evening from our visit with the Ashtar Command. This was my first experience with them and I have felt connected every since. Jesus or Sananda is in charge of this ship.

The next day was the end of the ascension seminar. When we were finished, one of the participants asked if we would like him to show us how to clear Axial Tonal lines. I had never heard of this. He asked me if I wanted to be on the table for the clearings. I said yes, not knowing what was to take place. It seems like I have been asked to be the one experimented on several times.

He explained to the others what he was going to be doing, so they could see the technique. Then he stated that he was told by the Masters of the Mountain to stand back and only hold the energies, for they were going to do the clearing. He said it surprised him to be told this, and he held the energies as they had asked him to do.

I knew St. Germain and Jesus were working on me, although after the session a clairvoyant mentioned there were many others Masters around the table. It was very intense. I was experiencing many different levels of energetic shifts, some very unpleasant, yet during rest periods, as they called them, I felt wonderful feelings of bliss. It was a special treat for me to have the Masters of the Mountain working on me. They were clearing all the energetic lines of places I had ever been in our Universe.

The facilitator mentioned that he hadn't seen someone who had connections to so many places. He also mentioned that the session is usually only one hour because of the intensity of the sessions, yet he witnessed all that was being done on me was around equivalent to three or four sessions combined in one sitting. He was very surprised.

I believe the Masters wanted all my clearings to be done all at once, which explains the intensity. When it was complete I sat up from the table and we discussed what others had seen and how they had learned something that was very unusual.

Some wanted to go up to the Mountain before dark. I said "Yes, I want to go too," again surprising the teacher, for one would normally have to rest for hours after this type of session. I got up, we ate food, then up to the Mountain we went. I wasn't even tired. I wonder what the Masters had done to have me recover so quickly. I felt great.

The next day my friends were working on each other and I felt like going out on the patio to relax and have time for myself. I was looking at our majestic Mountain, Mt. Shasta, when I went out of my body and was actually transported into the inner city of Telos by the Masters. I really don't remember what happened in the Mountain. The next thing I knew, I was being awakened by my friends, saying it was time to head home. I thought I had drifted off for only a few minutes when I was actually with the Masters almost two hours. Whatever took place in the Mountain I must have had a great time, as I woke up rested and feeling wonderful.

What an amazing adventure during and after our Ascension class. I was never the same after that; lots of changes were beginning to happen in my life.

Solara: January 11, 1991

I have always been a spiritual person. Even though I kept this aspect of myself hidden at times for personal reasons, still it seemed that I was always in the right place at the right time. I began to understand that part of my mission here on our beloved Mother Earth is to help bring in higher frequencies onto the planet.

I was called forth by my Divine I-Am Presence to be a part of this gathering. Assisting in anchoring these frequencies is very important in these moments in time.

During these times, the world was preparing for a great "shift" into another Timeline, an energy shift for Mother Earth as well as all of us evolving on the earth. Preparations have been in motion since the Harmonic Conversion in 1978. The codes began to appear daily on clocks that would read "11:11" and remind people.

Assisting in grounding and anchoring these energies created one of the biggest shifts in my body. This was the "Big Shift" that Solara and others had been preparing to anchor in for a long time. It was an honor to be part of the wonderful group.

Tachi-Ren: Angelic Walk-in, 1991

The leader and my friend from our 11:11 group called and asked me if I wanted to drive over to the redwoods on the coast with her. Tachi-Ren, a walk-in who had recently arrived here from the Angelic Realm, was going to teach a weekend class. I didn't know what it was about, but it was enough to hear that we would be on the coast with the redwoods working with an Angelic walk-in!

This experience with Tachi-Ren was the most far-out journey I had ever experienced. I thought I had seen so much already. Nothing came close to meeting Tachi-Ren. The teaching was titled "What Is Light Body?" She spoke much of the time using the "Language of Light," the language of the Angelic Realm. Wow! It sounded so odd to me at first, yet somehow I understood everything she was saying! My body went through shift after shift that entire weekend.

One day when we had some free time I took a walk in the amazing, beautiful redwoods. It made me so joyful. Then, all of a sudden, I was enveloped in this field of energy that today I know as a "vortex." Sounds stopped, time stopped. It seemed like everything stopped, a suspended moment in time! It was so beautiful and serene to be in this space.

When I began walking on the trail once more I realized I had been in this space to communicate with my special sixth-dimensional Big Foot friends. I was very excited to feel their energies again; it had been quite a while since we had communicated.

That evening we were outside by the fire when Tachi-Ren asked us if we would like to contact Big Foot. I got so excited; I couldn't wait to have this experience with the group. But honestly there wasn't much that came from the evening, at least not compared to my own time with them.

The next morning before we were leaving, Tachi-Ren gave each of us a personal reading. She told me that I came onto this planet as an Archangel. This was the first time I had actually heard these words spoken. It resonated with me as if I already knew this. More importantly, she said that I have a sixth-dimensional Big Foot group that has been working with me from a very early age. She also said they had been guiding me and would always be my guides to assist me whenever I needed them. All I would need to do is think of them and their presence would be with me.

Somehow this all made sense. I started to remember earlier times in the forest where they made their presence known to me. Even though I was too young to understand who they were, they were still there communicating with me. How blessed is that?

AnaKun: Clearing of Etheric Mt. Shasta

A friend called me, asking if I would like to be a part of a group going to Mt. Shasta with a spiritual teacher named AnaKun. She was a walk-in who had just arrived onto the planet. Wow, this was the second time I was meeting a walk-in within months. We were working in nature mainly in or around the forests in Big Foot country once more.

When we had just started out on the trail, my friend and I noticed a man was coming towards us. We said hello and smiled at each other. Something made us both turn around to look at him and he wasn't there! No one was on the trail and this was only a few moments after his passing by.

The trail was visible for a long way, so it wasn't like he went out of sight. He was gone, poof!

We asked ourselves, "Who was that?" We both got that it was a Master from Telos! Later, I was given information that it was Adama, the High Priest from Telos. How incredible to have him appear to say hello, then be gone!

This particular seminar required much more endurance and a higher level of work with Mother Earth then I had previously done.

The minute I looked at AnaKun I saw a "Wizard"! Yes, she looked just like a Wizard that you would see in the movies and she acted like one as well. I did find out after five days hiking and nights up on the Mountain that she really was a Wizard! She was unusually tall; a big woman with gray hair, looked like Merlin to me.

The first thing she said to us was, "We have to lighten our loads." I couldn't bring myself to leave my warm clothes and knew I had to have food, so I didn't lighten my load very much. We took our warm clothes, food and our sleeping bags to carry on our backs to hike miles up the Mountain. We hiked through snow, ice and cool weather before she found the place where we were to do our work. None of us at this time knew really what we were to do, except assist in clearing the astral layer of Mt. Shasta.

We weren't lying in the ice or snow, yet it was very cold! She proceeded to tell us we had to be more prepared to do this work, so she gave each of us Level 1 and 2 Reiki. She told us we had been together in Egypt as Priestesses and had agreed to come back at this time to do this work with Mt. Shasta. There were six of us present. On the way up, one participant decided she couldn't handle the journey. She got very upset with AnaKun and left.

This wasn't an easy journey. Sometimes there is one person in the group acting out elements that are within each of the other members. This was the case. She wasn't supposed to be with us for the entire time. She was there for the purpose of showing us what was inside us, only she was the one to act it out!

We did the work that AnaKun had prepared for us. It felt really good to me to be of such assistance to our beloved Mt. Shasta. After doing inner healing work and the long hike, it came time for us to go back down the Mountain. AnaKun said to us once more, "Lighten your loads." Let me tell you, my friend, I did just that. I wasn't going to carry anything more on my back, physically or symbolically. So she and I put our sleeping bags, our sweats and sweatshirts along with the food we had left into a tree high enough that hopefully bears wouldn't find it.

As were getting closer to the end of our trail, AnaKun said she was supposed to meet Gary Zukav during her visit. Only minutes after stating this, who do we meet coming up the trail but Gary and his girlfriend Linda. She knew them right away and took Linda aside to give her the Level 1 and 2 Reiki. She then mentioned what we were doing on the Mountain. Gary said he'd like to have us come over to his house for dinner the following night to celebrate what we had just done.

When we arrived at Gary's home the next day, we were surprised to see so many beautiful people. He invited many healers and before dinner they put us into the middle of the circle and everyone honored what we had done to heal the Astral Plane of our Beloved Mountain. Wow! What an evening, so unexpected...like everything that happened in those five days with AnaKun, the Mountain and those lovely people.

It turned out that the next year AnaKun changed her name to Isis. She called me to discuss the idea of bringing people to Kealakekua Bay to help clear layers of discordant energies. Of course I would help with the clearing!

We went by boat to do the ceremony at the bay; the dolphins were there and seemed to know what we were doing. It was so beautiful to be working with these higher Beings of Light, the dolphins and the people, to help clear the waters and energies of the bay.

Isis asked me if I wanted my third degree Reiki level. I was thrilled to be able to have Isis give me the Reiki 3 and Master level at the same time. She took me to the Green Valley Temple on the island and instructed me. All of this was completely unexpected, it just manifested into my reality. How I love being here and having these experiences that happen in the moment!

Patricia Cota-Robles

Patricia Cota-Robles is another amazing spiritual teacher I studied with in the 1980s. What I learned, and began to share with others, was her teaching on the "Twelve Aspects of Deity." Namely, these are The Twelve Rays of Creation, the Twelve Archangels and their Qualities. I taught these classes for many years and still use this modality today. Working with and sharing the Twelve Rays was very rewarding for me.

It became clear: One aspect of my mission here is to assist the Planet in Anchoring Rays of Light.

Some years after studying with Patricia, I had the privilege of swim-guiding her group here in Kona. It was such an amazing experience to get to know Patricia on a whole other level; she is a real true Master in my opinion. She is one who inspires all to Be All They Can BE! The Divine Light is shining within her at all times. She is a blessing to All of Us.

Bali
The Feminine Madonna Blue Ray

In Bali with Patricia in 2005, I was very blessed to be a part of the bringing in of the Feminine Madonna Blue Ray. This was one of the most amazing and sacred moments that were conducted by the Heavenly Realms of Light. We were also privileged to have the Prince of Bali join us; he is a friend of my friend. What an incredible surprise!

The Prince even asked if we would like to spend the night at his castle! We each had our own incredible separate spaces, like what we call ohanas here in Hawaii. That was such a wonderful experience to share Patricia's event and time with the Prince!

The day of the event was beyond words! A few minutes before 11:11 am, Patricia played "Amazing Grace." We all sang with tears in our eyes as the company of Heaven's choir began to sing out as the clock read 11:11, the hour that the Feminine Madonna Blue Ray entered our beloved Mother Earth and the Soul of Gaia. I could hear the angelic realm so loudly that I began to cry. They descended around us, it was so beautiful and real!

Mother Mary and Archangel Gabriel assisted the ceremony. We anchored in the Madonna Blue Flame of the Feminine Ray. I was so touched by this special event that I stood up and shared what I was feeling. The most incredible thing happened: as I finished sharing, Patricia told everyone in the room that I had swim-guided her group years prior and said anyone interested in going to Hawaii to swim with the dolphins should see me during the break. This made my heart sing with such joy to be acknowledged in this way by Patricia.

The next day my friends and I decided to drive around the island. We stopped at a yoga resort to have lunch. From the next table I overheard people taking about dolphins. After eating, I went over to speak with them and they shared that their group had come to the resort and tried to meet the dolphins several times, yet when they got in the water the dolphins left.

I told them what I do in Hawaii and they asked me if I would stay and take them out. Unfortunately all the rooms were taken; however, the owner said that her partner was out of town and that her room would be available for us to stay in if I could take them out in the morning. I was so happy to hear we could stay and also that we would have an opportunity to see the dolphins.

It was a full moon and my friends and I were sitting near the water with this beautiful moon shining. It was a magical moment, to say the least. I went into meditation with the dolphins and asked them to come and join us tomorrow if this was the highest good for them and us. After I finished communing with them I turned around, and to my surprise, the rest of the group was sitting behind me; they were so quiet I didn't know they were there. I knew then that we were all in sync.

We asked four fishermen if they would take us out the next morning and they said yes. These were old, small fishing boats that held three people, yet they worked. I asked everyone to please meet me at the water before dawn. The dolphins had told me to start our journey on the water as the sun was rising over the sacred Mountain where the Feminine Madonna Blue Ray had been anchored into Bali and our beloved Mother Earth.

Everyone showed up while it was still dark. We did a meditation to align with the dolphins and loaded into our little fishing boats. As the sun began to rise up above the sacred Mountain, it was a sight that I will never forget! The energy coming from the Mountain and the sun was indescribable. A golden ray of light was leading the way, followed by hues of yellow, blue, orange and magenta. It felt like the sacred Mountain was blessing us with these amazing feminine energies. The light that was surrounding us felt electrical.

In the distance we could see leap after leap in the water, where huge pods of spotted dolphins greeted us. We followed them for a while until they slowed down. My friend and I slowly and quietly slipped into the water to see if they would stay. One pod went under us quickly. We got back in our boats and tried a second attempt much more slowly. They were becoming very curious about what we were doing. This time more came towards and under us, yet they kept swimming by.

They were swimming nearer to our boats now. I advised the group that the next time we had our chance everyone should quietly and slowly slip into the water to see what they would do. To our surprise, they slowed down and some circled around us. We didn't swim after them but rather just stayed together. It was a success, according to the owner of the resort. It was the first time in many attempts through the years that the dolphins came to the people.

I was told later that dolphin killings still were happening in that area. I believe this is why they didn't trust us at first. Plus, some of the local companies taking people out would let the swimmers in all at once, everyone jumping in with no respect for the dolphins. I would leave too!

This was a confirmation that the Feminine Madonna Blue Ray of transformation had activated the energy in Bali and all the other sacred Mountains around the world.

Sedona Vortex with Shawné

Some friends and I asked Shawné, a spiritual healer, to have a gathering in Sedona to learn about and experience vortexes helping us with our psychic development. Shawné lives in Sedona in a very sacred area near one of the vortexes called Bell Rock. I had stayed in her home before. It is an amazing energy that surrounds her home. She has experience with these energies and Beings of the Vortex. To spend five days experiencing all of these amazing electrical frequencies in the sacred areas around Sedona was so enlightening!

Every day black helicopters would fly over us. How did they know we were there? There were times when we were in places where no one could see us and they still would fly over us. The military knew we were working with very high frequencies of love and light! This was my first eye-opener to how our government was watching and keeping higher energies from being shared; they sure didn't want us doing what we were doing. I learned so much from this trip and really began to see why things are the way they are, especially in regards to our Secret Government and all those stopping the people from advancing and living in sovereignty as we are meant to do.

After we left Sedona we went down to Scottsdale to a very special event.

Metatron
Scottsdale, Arizona Solstice

I was in Scottsdale visiting a friend and she mentioned there was going to be a ceremony for the

Summer Solstice. I got very excited to walk the labyrinth she had on her land. It was very large. Before we began the walk I felt this very powerful energy come from the beautiful blue skies to the right of me. I quickly looked up and saw the most incredible unbelievable huge angel formed in the sky when only moments earlier the sky was crystal blue with no clouds. Immediately the words "Metatron" came out of my mouth!

Everyone looked, seeing this magnificent Angel. It looked like it was covering more than one half of that area of sky! Then as we looked around we noticed there had also appeared many smaller wispy cloud formations that were very Angelic; there are no words to totally describe what we were seeing. We proceeded to walk the spiral of the labyrinth in an altered state of bliss.

After the ceremony and a delightful lunch, my friends and I went to a bookstore. As we walked in, the owner came over to me, saying how glad she was that I had arrived. I must have looked surprised. I smiled, not knowing what she was talking about, and I guess from the look on my face she too was surprised. She said, the person who normally does the readings at the store was sick and I was the person she had been waiting for to do the readings. I was surprised and told her I had come with my friends and we were only looking around, I hadn't come to do readings.

She said "OK," looking perplexed, then walked away. Later, I was up at the counter to purchase some items and I mentioned how we had come from the ceremony and how this huge angelic being appeared that I had announced loudly as Metatron! She looked at me and pulled out a photograph of the same angel formation she had taken before she owned the store, saying this *was* Metatron! He had appeared before her saying she was to open a bookstore and he would help her to take care of everything that needed to be done. She said this was Metatron's store, and she felt that he had also sent me to the store to meet her or for whatever other reason I was there. All I knew was that it was a beautiful store with incredible energies filled with so much LOVE!

I had known of Metatron. This was the amazing beginning of my journey in connecting with the Lord of all the Angels. Wow, what a blessing this has been for me. He is always close by me even when he isn't in my thoughts, and I know that with only a thought of him, he is with me whenever I require assistance.

Chapter 6

Special Moments of Spiritual Reflections

New Millennium 2000 Celebration
The Whale Shark Swim

Author and whale shark

We had the most incredible gathering of so many people for this most special event on the planet. It was a New Millennium—year 2000! We had three boats going out for a week's seminar. The experiences with the dolphins were wonderful, plus the teachings and sharings joining all of us together.

Toward the end of the seminar a plane was hired to go out and spot the sperm whales, along with many fishermen who alerted us to let us know if they saw sperm whales. Our desire was to go out into the deeper blue waters to be with them, as they have this special energy that is in alignment with our New Beginnings. Unfortunately, we were unable to find the whales, so all three boats stopped in this pure, deep, blue water with the sun's rays flowing down into the waters—or were the rays of light flowing up from the bottom's deep abyss? Either way it was so beautiful. The silence was serene, the sun was warm and shining as we all floated and dove within these crystalline blue waters of Lemuria! So many memories came to mind and feelings of immense joy flowed through me. This was what was meant to be for our group; instead of finding sperm whales we were to have this experience of complete silence and serenity, peace being born into our Souls as we shared this time together. Lemuria became alive!

New Year's Day was our last day together, the First Day of my New Beginnings. My marriage of 33 years had just come to a close. We still loved one another, yet were no longer able to live together. We had both changed and needed something different in our lives.

This was the seminar of all seminars! We had a rare experience presented to us. Many participants and I were able to swim with a whale shark! This was a first for me; I had never swum with a whale shark before. It was one of the greatest experiences I've had the opportunity to take part in.

The amazing love that flowed from this beautiful being was a highlight in my explorations of the blue world of the ocean. It was a young whale shark, so gentle, just wanting to hang with the people. It would go from boat to boat, sometimes rubbing against the boat as if it was its mother. It seemed lonely and wanted company. At one point it glided right past me; I gently held my hand out a little from my side and it brushed against it. Oh, this was so loving. My heart filled with so much joy and blessings. I was so happy to be able to experience this beautiful being of love. It was a great heart-opening for me and continued in the coming months of 2000. What a gift to start the New Year!

Grandma Chandra
Kona, Hawaii 2003

2003 was another incredible life-altering year with many special shifts coming onto our beloved Mother Earth. This was the year that James Twyman brought the Indigo Children to Kona. They presented at a conference, sharing their gifts and knowledge. What a pleasure to listen and learn from these children of Light! Grandma Chandra was one that was also presenting. Grandma is a twelfth-dimensional being that is multiply handicapped, a pure channel of light that is from the eleventh dimension, a very powerful young woman.

In Kona on December 12, 2003, the 12:12 date, Grandma activated the "Stargate" or "Portal" between Mauna Kea and Mauna Loa, two of Hawaii's sacred mountains. This activated Lemuria and more of my memories! This activation brought in the "Sacred Mother Energy" to balance the male and female energies for all on the planet.

Grandma was told that a Kahuna would heal her in Hawaii. When her mother, Cat, attempted to get a hold of different Kahunas in Kona, it wasn't working out. This was confusing, for they had received the message that a Kahuna would heal her! One day on a private boat trip, many humpback whales appeared and one whale went right under the boat. Grandma said, "This is it: this is the Kahuna that is to heal me!"

After the trip Grandma began to walk with a walker; she hadn't walked before, and now she was able to get around by herself.

Grandma and I work together on the higher dimensions. She tells me she has come to me many times while I am with the dolphins and in Tonga with the humpback whales. She shape-shifts into one or the other depending on each cetacean I am swimming with.

One day our seminar group had a boat trip and after assisting them back on the boat I was drawn to go back in by myself to have an experience with the dolphins. One dolphin came directly toward me, we were nose to nose as it looked me in the eye. But its eye wasn't the eye of a dolphin; it was a human's eye! It kept with me for a while, transferring information into my soul. The dolphin felt like a dolphin, yet also human—what was this all about?

During the conference I was sitting in the front row with my good friends, when Grandma called on the person in the turquoise outfit to come up to the front. I felt that it was me she was calling on, but I felt shy so I didn't go up. Grandma's interpreter said, "Yes, YOU, please come up!" Oh my, I was so nervous, why call on me?

My friends practically pushed me to go up. When I got up there Grandma said, "You know that you are an Archangel don't you?" The words came out without even thinking as I replied, "Yes!" and started to cry. This was something I couldn't tell people, I was afraid of their judgments, like "Who does she think she is?" These were my own thoughts; I had always felt I would be judged if I told others who I knew I really was. Grandma said I had to admit this out loud so I could embody the essence that was mine, the angelic part of myself, and to stop hiding!

There were so many people in the audience. I heard many of my friends yell out, "We always knew that, Celeste!" I felt a big relief come over me, although this still isn't something I mention very often, unless I feel a deep connection to a person.

I was asked if I had a question for Grandma. I told the story about the dolphin/human eye experience on the boat trip and Grandma said, "Oh yes, that was me coming to share with you." When I had a chance to look her in the eyes I saw that it was true: those were the eyes of Grandma Chandra. She had shape-shifted into the dolphin! I have since seen her eyes while with the humpback whales. She is so clever to visit me through the dolphins and whales; we both love them so much.

She had my Omni Chamber made for me. The energy of this device allows a person sitting under it to be taken to or experience the 33rd dimension; this is how powerful the pyramid is. It looks like a pyramid although it is much more, and extremely powerful. It is for manifesting and healing and also enables other higher-dimensional qualities to be received. It sits outside my bedroom; I am constantly experiencing these sacred frequencies as a normal part of my life. Thank you Grandma for your friendship and love.

Joan's Portal Seminar 2003
Babaji and the Portal

In August 2003 I was assisting Joan Ocean with her two-week "Portal Seminar." This seminar was to open and enter the Portal here in Hawaii. We had 44 participants: a perfect number for the work we would be doing. Each day we built on the next to prepare ourselves for the grand day of entering the Portal. It was quite an amazing preparation.

On the day of the Portal, I woke up early morning to my precious dog Babaji sneezing blood. He was hemorrhaging and blood was everywhere. I quickly got him to the vet, who said he would have to watch him for a while. I had to leave, for I was supposed to go and pick up participants who were staying at the hotel. It was still too early and I was so scared for my dog that I went straight up to Joan's. A few people who were staying at Joan's saw the blood all over me. I was so upset I had trouble explaining what had happened. Joan came out and asked me if I could please stay and tell the others who were on their way what had happened as everyone was very concerned.

Once everyone had arrived we went down to our meeting area and Joan had me sit beside her in front of the group. She asked me to tell everyone what had happened.

As I began to explain, my sweet little Babaji's energy came from the vet hospital. He was bringing his message through me to explain why and for what reason he had started hemorrhaging. I really don't remember anything said, for it was Babaji who was telling the story. When I opened my eyes tissues were being passed around the room, I didn't see a dry eye in the group! People began to share what they felt. So many heart-filled blessings were shared for my sweet Babaji and myself, I too began to cry. All the sharings were special to me, but the most touching feelings came from Jean Luc, who is part-owner with Joan and lives on the Sky Island Ranch. He said he had never cried before, even when he had lost his own pet, and he now had tears! That meant so much to me.

Joan quickly said, "It's time to enter the Portal!" This is what it took for everyone, all 44 of us, to be in a deep state of love and compassion; these were the requirements to enter the Portal. With the assistance of my beloved Babaji we all were in this state of grace, so we could enter. I must say, everyone was filled with love and compassion!

One participant mentioned that while my dog Babaji was speaking through me, she saw the "man Babaji" behind me the entire time. Wow, I guess that may have had an impact on achieving that state that was required.

I found a precious dog in a box in front of a grocery store after my wonderful dog of twelve years passed away. I was so sad and when I saw this little puppy, I knew I had to have him. He was very unusual looking: he had the body of a yellow lab, yet he had a tiny sweet face and his legs were very short for such a lab body.

When I got him home, the first thing he started doing was running around making me laugh. The rest of our time together, around 12 years, he was like my court jester, especially when I felt sad about anything. I asked him what his name was and he said "Babaji." At the time, I didn't know about the man Babaji. At first I called him by this name, until I could see that most of my family and my small granddaughter couldn't say the name, so for many years I called him "Bobbie" to make it easier for everyone else. I forgot that he wanted to be called his master name!

It wasn't until he started getting well from the sad day of his hemorrhaging that he told me I must call him by his real name, Babaji. As soon as I started calling him his real name he started getting better and lived another four years. It was all about the vibration in his name that he could become the master that he was. The animals tell us and teach us so much, don't they? I know I learn from them every day—from my dogs, the dolphins and whales, and many other special beings that are here to share with us.

Light Transmission and Transference
TILAK: Man of Light and Wisdom

My present leap from illusionary reality onto the path of liberation was when I met Tilak in 2003. So who is Tilak? He is a man who is REAL AND TRANSMITS LIGHT, creating openings for the individual to move to their next level of evolution if they choose. You are able to truly see your own light, to see your real authentic self, with these third eye openings. You drop your veils and boundaries through this process.

I have received many intensives and I am presently doing a more expanded intensive, which has brought me into my knowingness without doubts or fears! It is so gratifying to know and feel all your aspects of Self beginning to merge and be in harmony with your present moment. I have changed so much since having Tilak in my life; I can truly say that my physical body has gone through many shifts with the veils being dissolved. It is quick and transformative in every way, and this has been what my life is about at this present moment.

Master Sha: 2008

I met Master Sha in Mt. Shasta in 2008. He wasn't known yet. He gave a transmission to the audience that shook my world. It was amazing, the power that he transmitted to us. I invited him to come to Kona to give a transmission at the Aloha Theater. I picked him up from the airport and when we reached our destination and I parked the car he asked me to stay. He had been giving a lesson on his cell phone as I was driving, which I have to say was a little difficult with the energy he was transmitting to those in his class. When he gave the command "Download," my car shock from side to side. I opened my eyes, for I thought someone was pushing my car back and forth. No one was there; it all came from his energy and the power of the transmission he was delivering!

Master Sha gave healing transmissions to the audience that evening that everyone seemed to enjoy. He started a Sunday free healing class for one hour to those who chose to have healings or blessings. I then signed up and took many of his online classes to become a Soul Healer. Before the oral exam I had with Master Sha to complete my courses, I decided that I had to do my own healing work. Interestingly, this information came to me from the whales after I returned from my Tonga trip; they wanted me to create and do my own original healing work from the many gifts of special teachers in my life, most importantly the angels, dolphins and whales! This was my mission, to receive information from them in the Present Moment as well as from the Teachers of Light and Masters. Master Sha was a gift in my life, and from him I learned the Tao, which has been very helpful in my healing practice.

Trip to France, 2008
Mary Magdalene

In 2008 Mary Magdalene came in very strong and began to communicate with me as if I was speaking with a long-lost friend from the past. It was as if we had been together only yesterday. It was so comfortable to share information with Mary. She felt like an older sister giving me knowledge that she herself had already gone through and benefited by. I was learning so much.

A few months before leaving for my Tonga whale trip, she asked or almost told me I was to go to France to learn about her, and more importantly, to assist in healing and brightening light in sacred sites where she once lived and taught. She said there were darker energies in places that she would like for me to uplift with light!

I told my friend Connie what I was to do. Connie is very close to Mother Mary and said she would like to go too. It was so nice to have a friend on this journey. We began to plan the trip right after my return from Tonga.

A week after my annual Tonga trip, Connie and I flew into Paris, arriving on September 30, 2008. We spent a few days going to places that Mary asked me to visit. I loved going to the Louvre and seeing all the beautiful paintings, especially one of Mary Magdalene, Jesus and Mother Mary. The *Mona Lisa* gave me shivers also. Then we went to our hotel in downtown Paris and slept for hours.

I was awoken with spirit saying to me that I must complete my past relationships in this lifetime before I could move forward in my life. Connie received similar guidance.

Our room number was 9, symbolizing completion, and no accidents there! I am very into numbers and their significance in relation to what I am doing. What we didn't realize was the financial crisis in the world had just begun and big changes were happening inside as well as outside of me.

I was on a quest for my spiritual evolution, with Mary Magdalene, Jesus and Mother Mary energies guiding me all the way. This journey was about me activating the codes of Mary Magdalene. It seemed as if I was returning to my true heritage of Mary Magdalene and Jesus.

We took a train ride to Southern France; this was primarily where she wanted me to be. We stayed at Les Labadous, a Cathar house, in the Languedoc area, yet at first I didn't realize the owner was a practicing Cathar. Our window looked out to Rennes-le-Château, which is dedicated to Mary Magdalene. It is in the heart of sacred geometry and compels change.

It was mystical to see the complexity of this sacred town. It held the power point by the Lemurians, who were aware of it. What makes it a portal, an angelic attractor, is the crystalline structure of the geology—primarily the Mountains—which is amplified by geometry. It is the crystalline structure of the rocks that holds light in a peculiar way and it draws all manner of energy beings and angels.

The next morning we were having breakfast when Japp, the owner of the retreat, started telling us stories about Mary Magdalene. These were tales he remembered as a boy, as he was a Cathar. These stories were told and handed down through his lineage. He had written three books about Mary in Dutch.

Japp knew of places that were sacred and unknown to many and offered to take us. He asked if I knew I was a Cathar and I said, "Yes, I have known I was a Cathar." This is the reason he was sharing so much with me.

One of my favorite places to visit was the two sacred Mountains. The female Mountain is called Pech Cardou and the male sacred Mountain is called Bugarach. Amazing energies of the female and male, Mary Magdalene and Jesus—lots of relationship energies in Southern France that were needing to be rebalanced.

He told us the Bugarach Mountain is where they say the Arc of the Covenant is buried and where UFOs enter. This sacred Mountain felt a lot like Mt. Shasta, where I grew up: very mystical and magical.

Out our driveway behind the pillar was the Temple of Lemurians. Japp called this valley the "Valley of the Milky Way," a very sacred area. As we gazed out into this canyon, it really did resemble our Milky Way. When I took pictures on this sacred site, all my pictures had many beautifully colored Orbs, mainly blue and pink, male and female! I took many pictures of the sun while standing on the plateau and the geometries and orbs were incredible!

We could also see the plateau from our room, as it was right below Rennes-le-Château, which was so beautiful and breathtaking. One day we walked to the plateau and I began having visions of a village and actually felt and saw Mary Magdalene living in this village. I sensed also that Jesus had presence there.

The tower on the plateau is the "Tour Visigoth." Here is a sacred fountain with the four lions on each corner. A short distance away is a pillar with two doves looking at each other. I believe these doves signify Mary Magdalene and Jesus as "in love and married." This plateau is also said to be the last of the Lemurian civilization of 30,000 to 40,000 years ago.

One night at dinner we were graced with a couple that came to visit Japp. They started talking about the Cathars, and Alan, a present-day practicing Cathar, said they had been invited by Japp to come from Germany.

When dinner was over Alan mentioned he knew I was a Cathar and would like to give me the Cathar's Prayer that is only handed down through the lineages. I got very excited and we proceeded into a beautiful room with a blazing fire. What an amazing setting in which to receive this oral tradition. He recited the prayer to me, as I could only write it down; it is only for a Cathar to receive this prayer. How privileged I felt to receive this prayer. An evening I'll never forget, remembering where I came from, my lineage from France.

The next morning Japp took Alan, his wife, Connie and me to the cave of Mary Magdalene. It was wonderful to enter into the womb or the birthing cave where women would come to give birth, Mary being the midwife. Next to this cave is where Mary lived, possibly with Jesus and their children at times. It is said that they also lived across this area on the plateau below Rennes-le-Château. I used this birthing cave to ask the Divine, Mary Magdalene, Jesus and Mother Mary to take away my pain, frustrations and sorrows. I went out of the cave through the birth canal to my new life or rebirth. It is said others would come for healings at times. Japp, our guide, said he felt he was a child during Mary's time here; this is why he is acquainted with the inner knowledge about this area. He also said that Rennes-le-Château and Pech Cardou are sister Mountains that represent Isis, the female energy, while Burgarch is Osiris, the male energy. Pech Cardou is said to have 12 entrances, and the Temple of Solomon lies beneath it. Japp said it could possibly have Mary and Jesus buried there as well, as everything may be concealed deep underground.

One day we visited the Magdalene Church at Rennes-le-Château. It was not that exciting for me; it felt dark and some of the statues were scary looking. I didn't need to spend a lot of time in that particular church. They believe that a subterranean crypt was part of an ancient Temple of Isis, who was the restorer of eternal life. Part of the mystery of Mary Magdalene was her training as a priestess of Isis. It seemed to me that this was one of the sacred places that Mary wanted me to transmit some "light" into. Of all our sites visited, this was the least enjoyable place, but since there was a lot of darkness and it needed light, it made sense that I would be feeling uneasy.

After visiting the church, we decided to get some lunch, so we ventured down the street to the "Restaurant la Table de l'Abbe." We entered a wonderful courtyard, sitting down at a beautiful area near a fountain. We sat there for some time without being waited on, so we went up to the counter and asked if someone would take our order. It was as if we had become invisible to the waitress. A man named Toby said he would be right over. Toby turned out to be the owner and he asked if we had been to the Cathar Castle in Aude, called Peyrepertuse. Peyrepertuse originated in 1050 and is the largest of all fortresses in Aude. After being at the forefront of the battles opposing the last defenders of Catharism and the royal army, it still had strategic importance for many years.

It was early evening when Toby took me up to the castle and it was starting to get dark. No one wanted to walk up the wooden planks to get to the top of the entrance to the castle, which was very steep. I knew we would have to come down in the dark with only our flashlights, yet I knew I was supposed to go, so Toby and I went up. I couldn't believe the feelings that were coming into my awareness as we entered the difficult entrance. He had to boost me up just to get to the entrance.

Once inside I looked down into this courtyard and immediately had the vision that I was there. It used to be so festive, a place where people gathered to celebrate and enjoy food and games. It was a beautiful courtyard before we were forced to hold up in the fortress due to the Catholic Church's crusade to kill all Cathars. They weren't able to control the teaching that Mary

Magdalene was continuing after Jesus's actual death at an old age. This is the only way they could control us, by killing us.

This has gone on throughout the world from the beginning of time. The same religious issues are being fought over and over. It will never end until everyone decides to put down their guns and stop warring with each other. The only way this can happen in this timeline is for the warring to stop within ourselves. I saw myself being there at the very end and witnessing many being burned by their own free will in order not to be slaughtered by the Church. It was an amazing vision for me to see and to remember more of my heritage in France.

Before we made our journey to the castle, Toby invited us to have lunch at his home down the street from his restaurant. It was between the Magdalene Church and the Templar Castle.

He welcomed us into his home and as I entered the doorway, I felt very different. I wasn't sure why at the time. He took us out into his courtyard in the back and Gerta, his wife, had set up a wonderful lunch at a table outside with a couple of their guests, who we learned were all practicing Templars. An amazing experience was unfolding. We found out their home was once owned by priest Beranger Sauniere, who dedicated the church to Mary Magdalene. During a renovation, he discovered the famous documents that reveal the true identity of Mary Magdalene and the sacredness of the feminine. He later built the Tower of Magdala in her honor, which overlooks the sacred plateau that was once a village in the vision that was given to me. Henry Lincoln's book *Holy Blood, Holy Grail* was a major source of information for Dan Brown's writing and movie *The Da Vinci Code*.

After our lunch, we started on our journey for a tour of Alet-les-Bains, the medieval town. There, Toby showed us evidence of the Templars. The most interesting place was the home of Nostradamus's grandparent. Before the door hung a large carving of different symbols proving his grandfather was a Templar and possibly the Prior of Sion. Those who knew about the Templars also knew the symbols' meaning. While looking at these symbols and hearing Toby's explanations regarding them, I felt I too knew what they were saying to those who had the privilege and opportunity to be able to be there.

We stopped at a very old church; it was one of the oldest Templar churches. Toby had to have special permission to get a key for us to go in, he being in the order of the Templars. It had amazing statues. The red cross on a white background is the Templar symbol. This was such an amazing day, especially with the day ending at the Cathar Castle, as I was remembering so much of my time in France on another timeline.

A short drive from Rennes-le-Château, we visited a most amazing Angel art gallery and sanctuary. I have never seen such beautiful rooms filled with mystical paintings of angels by the artist and owner named Lorraine. I felt like I knew her immediately and told her my middle name was Lorraine, creating an instant bonding between us I couldn't explain. During the war in France, my dad's favorite town where he stayed was called Lorraine. He wanted my middle name to be Lorraine. Here I was in France meeting Lorraine, and the spelling is the same. She told me Lorraine means "The Victorious One," and has reference to the "Laurel plant" in relationship to

Jesus. That was no surprise to me.

Her three-year-old daughter came outside while we were sitting and talking. As she was approaching us I thought I was seeing myself. She looked just like I did at that age, hair and eye color just the same! She said she was a fairy, and I said, "Yes, I know. I am one too!" Her eyes lit up and we both hugged each other, laughing. It was wonderful to connect with my human angelic family in France.

We had spent eight lovely days in Southern France even though they were filled with very intense energies. I felt complete as I left this area. I did what I had come to do. I was to walk the area of my past heritage, not so much to take these energies within myself, but more to give "light" to the old energies no longer serving myself and others. These energies were to be transformed into light from the older dark energies from the past.

I felt very blessed to have been able to have the visions and feelings of love from the Cathars and the Templars. October 13 was to be a big day, especially at Burgarach, being the day that they were killed by the Roman Catholic Church. I felt that we didn't need to be there for this event; it was time for us to head to Sainte-Maries-de-la-Mer, where Mary Magdalene had arrived with her daughter and others in France. We visited the church of the Two Maries and the Effigy of Sarah, the black statue of the daughter of Mary and Jesus. In this wonderful setting, you say a prayer by lighting a candle. It was beautiful and inspirational.

After spending almost a week on the French Riviera, we headed back to spend our last few days in Paris. We attended a wonderful Sunday service at the Notre Dame Church. Then we walked to the Church of St. Sulpice, which is related to Mary Magdalene and the Magdalene meridian line that runs all the way up from Southern France in Rennes-le-Château, where we had stayed. Our last evening was at the Eiffel Tower, so amazing with the lights of Paris below us.

I am grateful to Mary Magdalene for assisting me on my adventure in regard to her mission in France, as well as the mission and adventure that she, Jesus and Mother Mary guided me on so beautifully. I learned so much about myself and why I am here. Thank you, my beloved hosts, for your Presence with me during my sacred journey to France. I was enlightened and inspired to be more of who I Am!

Braco, the Gazer
January 2010

It was time for me to study my own healing methods from my own Soul/Spirit after Master Sha's teachings. I knew I didn't need to have another teacher brought in to teach me things. I was my own Teacher!

In 2010, my friend Angelica sent me an email with information about a man who "gazes" and assists in healing people in Croatia, his home country. He would see thousands of people each day and amazing healings were happening from his gazing alone, without him speaking or touching others.

As I looked into his eyes in the photo on the email, they mesmerized me! There was something very different about Braco. My body recognized this energy, even though I wasn't sure why. Angelica traveled to Croatia and spent 21 days with Braco, then came back and wrote a book in a short period of time. She invited him to our transformational conference in January 2010 and he accepted.

Before he arrived, Angelica decided to bring a few together to be an experimental group on Skype to see what healings could happen.

The first time, many of us stood in front of the computer and Braco started gazing and the most miraculous thing happened! First I saw a golden white aura around his head! I don't see auras, yet I saw this one around him! I had neck problems from a car accident years before that would give me challenges now and then. When he started gazing, a warm light came out from the computer and, like a laser, went to my neck where it was hurting. This was the first of many amazing healings I received from Braco.

January 8th was the first time I met Braco in person. We took him to the beach to swim, acting as a bodyguard in some ways, as to allow him to enjoy himself without people coming up to speak to him. He was no longer speaking with the people, he was only gazing. It was a very interesting time and experience, to say the least!

His first live gaze was on January 11th. It was so incredible to have him stand in front of a large crowed and gaze, while people received whatever was for them to receive. The energy was so high, my heart filled with so much love. Again, I was able to see an aura around him, this time in person. Many others also mentioned that they too had never experienced seeing aura's before. At times he would shape-shift into other faces. It is indescribable and it is such an individual experience.

I experienced his frequencies as Christ energies. I was blessed and fortunate to be able to be on staff here in the islands, touring Maui and Honolulu from the Big Island, where it all began. I was privileged to know Braco as a man who does speak like anyone else; matter of fact, he is quite funny and so loving. I have never met a man and healer, although he doesn't like being called a healer, who can transmit energies from a gaze. This defies scientific explanation and conventional understanding; the power of Braco's gaze miraculously heals the body and empowers people in their lives. This is a man whose life embodies a perfect balance between the spiritual and the material world we live in.

After our last session of the day, the staff would start walking and find a place to eat. It was in the moment, never planned. We always found the best places without knowing where we would end up. I learned so much just from these experiences, staying in the moment, allowing the perfect place to manifest for us. A couple of times Braco would do some really silly things at dinner. What fun times we had. After dinner we would walk the beach in Honolulu before bedtime, talking and laughing, enjoying each other's company. Those were amazing inspirational times of evolving ourselves with love, light, compassion, and pure joy of Being!

Aside from meeting and knowing Braco, a treasured experience, the highlight for me was when Braco gazed for us here in Kona, Hawaii through New Year's Eve into the New Year of 2012. Wow, how does it get any better than this? When he does come to Kona to gaze I feel so wonderful to be able to go up to him and greet Braco as my brother, a very special friend. What a gift he is in my life.

13th Crystal Skull Activation

During Trish's seminar we were graciously gifted the opportunity to have a private session with Susan, who is the keeper of the 13th crystal skull at the Shambhala Center in Mt. Shasta. This crystal skull is so little it fits in the palm of your hand; I expected a larger skull like most of the rest of the skulls. It is said that once the 13th skull was found, it would activate all the other skulls. Susan took the skull around the group, and as she did it would change colors! It would even breathe and shift what it looked like, depending on how Susan held it. We were very blessed to experience the energy of the skull in our hand, heart and third eye.

She said it would activate other crystals. I had my Lemurian crystal on and put it over my heart as she activated my heart chakra and physical heart. When I got back to Kona, I was swimming with the dolphins and began to tell a circle of my friends about my Mt. Shasta trip and the 13th crystal skull. Then, people across from me watched my Lemurian crystal begin to change colors just as the skull had done. Wow, it was really true: my crystal had been activated! I then was able to activate my Tonga Whale group's Lemurian crystals that were generously gifted to each participant by my special friend Candy.

Birthing Golden Lemuria
March 2011

In March 2011, a wonderful seminar took place here in Kona with special facilitators, Grandma Chandra, Judith Moore and Laurie Anderson. This amazing gathering was called the "Birthing of the Golden Lemuria." When I first heard the word "Lemuria," I knew I was to be there! We spend the first few days listening to the speakers. Then we went to different sacred sites to do activations on the Kona side of the island. It was interesting that when we were in ceremony at the volcano with Pele, steam began to spout up from the cauldron when there hadn't been any before. Even more interesting was when Pele would blow from the crater, it sounded like the very loud blows when the whales surface for air, blowing out their breath from a dive. After the ceremony I mentioned this to the Kahuna, as well as others, and they also agreed it sounded like whales. I felt they were there with us. We still had some of humpback whales in the area; mostly moms and calves were making themselves known to us, being a part of our group.

Another day the group ventured up north to the petroglyphs for our first ceremony to activate this area. We each picked a petroglyph to stand on during the ceremony. When we were complete, Judith and I were walking to another area that was a huge field of petroglyphs. All of a sudden I saw this was an area where UFO ships come and go. I mentioned this to Judith, adding that the beings from the ships helped the Hawaiians to make these petroglyphs. She said she was also getting that same message. As we were walked back to our cars Judith mentioned that Grandma Chandra wasn't feeling up to coming that day, yet had told Judith to have ME anchor in the "Crystalline Whale Codes" for humanity. Without hesitation I said "Yes I will," not knowing how this was to come about; it just came out of my mouth!

Judith got out a map and as I was looking at it, I felt the activation would be somewhere near Puako, where I had spent time with whales. They loved that area. We stopped at a special place in the area where the whales hang out and decided to have our lunch. We hadn't had much time to share among ourselves since there had been little free time. We started sharing, and when a person is sharing it is polite to acknowledge them while they are speaking. There was a small space between the trees where you could see the water. I wasn't facing the water. All of a sudden this energy of light came to me like a laser. I was trying very hard to listen to the person speaking at the same time, but thank goodness a girl yelled out, "Whale!"

We all got up ran to the shoreline. Way out, a mothers whale's tail was slapping over and over. It reminded me of the mother whale in Tonga that gave me blessings and her frequencies. She was doing the same as this whale.

Judith looked at me and said, "Is it time?" I said, "Yes!" The minute I put out my hand towards the whale, a bolt of light came through my arm, and the next thing I knew I was sounding out very loudly the message Mother Whale wanted to transmit through me to the 144,000 crystalline grids of our beloved Mother Earth, into her Soul, Gaia. I am not one who typically delivers a message like this through sounds, but she wanted me to share the information in this form to the group.

After the sounds stopped I put my hand up towards the heavens and heard my voice say, "We are now in the Galaxy, we are among the stars, it is so beautiful, magical and mystical." I felt the Galaxy within me and it was asking us all to bring the heavens and all the stars into our bodies. I placed my hand on the ground and pushed my hand hard onto the earth, anchoring the "Divine Crystalline Whale Codes" for humanity into the 144,000 crystalline grids of our beloved Mother Earth, into her Soul, Gaia. What an incredible blessing for us from this the beautiful mother whale who was the spokesperson for all the whales.

Patricia Cota-Robles, August 2011
Harmonic Convergence

I was listening to Patricia talk regarding the Shift of the Ages. I would like to quote some of the things she mentioned: "We are getting assistance from the Beings of Light, the whole of Creation, we are being breathed back, all life on the planet is moving from third, fourth to fifth dimensions, we are bringing the whole of Creation, we will never have to go through this again." The Beings of Light said, "At this moment in time, through all the realms, the greatest privilege is physical embodiment, the new octave of Divine Love."

11.11.11

Deborah Donohue asked me to facilitate the dolphin swims for her group for the week of the 11:11, November 11, 2011. We were heading up north to find the dolphins and discussing my whale trip to Tonga. Then we began to see whales in the distance. Just by talking about the whales, our energy was focused on them, and they were letting us know where they were. As we focus on something, most likely it will appear.

I continued sharing about a dolphin friend named Trusty, who assisted in my experiencing all the twelve dimensions of time, when out of nowhere appeared a large bottlenose dolphin at the bow of our boat, leading us somewhere. Our boat was traveling at a very high speed. It was amazing to see this dolphin move at the bow so fast, now and then looking up at us! The dolphin told me he was a Kahuna Dolphin, bringing us into Oneness. Wow, it was incredible to watch this Kahuna show us the way.

At some point he moved off and disappeared as quickly as he appeared. We had an outstanding swim with many dolphins who greeted us and swam with us for hours, sharing their love and healing abilities with those who were present. Then I went to my friends' group, led by Trish and Doug, to transmit the Crystalline Whale codes. The Angels sang and shared in the blessings that the whales were transmitting to us!

Activated Whale Codes

Trish and Doug had asked me to be their guest speaker at their seminar for the 11:11. Their event was held outside in a beautiful lawn area where you could hear the ocean's serenade to us. Clear warm weather filled the air.

First, the harp ensemble Anela Strings began playing their harps with inspiring angelic music, opening and filling our hearts with love. They were opening our energetic channels to receive the magnificent crystal whale codes that a beloved mother whale had transferred to me here in Kona earlier that year.

This was the second group to which I was given permission to transfer the whale codes. The first was my Tonga group that September, where we created a "Lemurian Portal of Light" with the assistance of the whales and our Sirian ship that was stationed above us.

The crystalline whale codes were given to each participant with the highest blessings from the whales that encircle our Beloved Mother Earth. Gaia, the soul of our Mother Earth, flowed up into each person as the Sirian energies flowed down to each one of the participants. It is very powerful to receive these codes, yet they are only transferred by permission from the Council of One, from my Sirian ship. So sweet was this day.

All around the world people were celebrating the 11:11 event. It was to be celebrated for the next 11 days of harmony and abundance at 11:11 for 11 minutes.

I had just gotten home from having the whales magnetically pull me up to Hawi from Ho'okena, a two-hour drive I wasn't expecting to do when I'd left the house early that morning.

I went to all the bays thinking I would swim with the dolphins. Instead, after standing at the Ho'okena lookout, the whales' magnetic field merged with mine and I knew I was to go to the other end of the island where they are coming in from Maui. I didn't even stop by my house on the way but continued driving up to Mauna Kea park, past Hawi.

I found a point where I could see a long distance and allowed my body to become a vessel for the whales. I expanded so far it felt like infinity. A huge amount of "Light Quotient" flowed through me and prepared me to receive our new "Mer Ka Na" Light Body, our crystalline stellated icosahedron (see graphic below), a 20-pointed dual inner rotation with double infinity flows! Our new Mer Ka Na Light Body rotation is an infinity flow!

Interesting to note that the icosahedron is one the cosmic solids and it represents WATER, LIQUID, FEMALE AND BEGINNING OF THE NEW CONSCIOUSNESS! Everyone on our beloved Mother Earth is receiving this today!

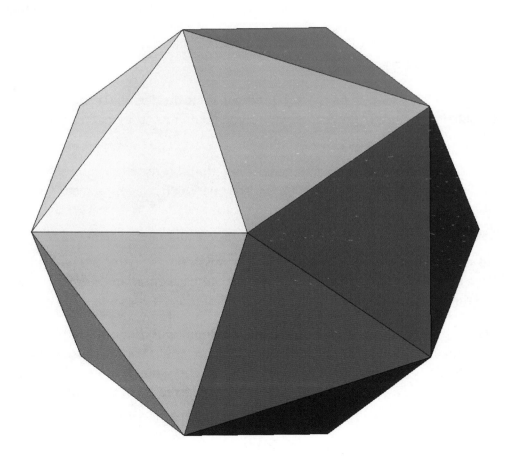

Icosahedron

Solar Eclipse, Mt. Shasta, March 2012

The most powerful shift for me to date was on the Solstice in March 2012.

I was called to go to Mt. Shasta for the total solar eclipse. My intention was to meet a few friends and experience this in a small group. It turned out that I was guided to participate in an event that was facilitated by Aluna Joy and Troika St. Germain. I learned a lot from these two wonderful people. We spent days leading up to the solar eclipse preparing and receiving knowledge from the Mayan Elders, from St. Germain as well as other Beings of Light. The day of the eclipse it was so beautiful outside: clear blue skies with a few wispy angel clouds and our wondrous majestic Mt. Shasta in her full Presence of Being!

We gathered in a baseball field with safety glasses, awaiting the eclipse to begin. I looked behind, and to my excitement, sitting to the side of our massive snow-covered Mountain was a Mother Ship awaiting this special event just as we were! I was trying to figure out how I was going to look at both the sun and the Mountain at the same time. Both the sun and the Mountain were transmitting high-energy frequencies to all of us in between the two of them! This was over-the-top energetically, as the sun's eclipse, the mother ship and our beloved Mountain were shifting all the cells in our bodies. How could it get any better than this? It was the ultimate heart and soul opening to this date, elevating and evolving us once more. What a wondrous reality we live in.

November 20, 2012: Solar Eclipse

This Solar Eclipse gives us Pluto, a spiritual world healing, Chiron, a personal healing, and Vesta, a heart healing. Also Juno, the north node, moves us into right relationship with Pleiades, the new humans being born each 25,560 years after December 21, 2012. Hawaii is anchoring the polarity alignment of our pituitary gland in the brain to our spiritual knowing. Pele's sacred intention flows into all the other sacred sites. The 19.5-degree latitude of Lemuria is the tetrahedron grid, the Rainbow Female Dragon line through the South Pacific. Here any remnants of female energy will rise up to find their place into beauty, love, and all the feminine qualities. Mexico is the mouth of the dragon; this is where all the teaching starts.

12.12.12

Deb Donohue returned the next year for December 12, 2012, the 12:12 event. Again, I was invited to swim-guide her group with the dolphins. It was so interesting, as we were leaving the harbor Deb asked me to speak to the group after she talked about the 12:12 activation. I said yes, and as she and I were speaking to the group a person asked about the whales. I started to talk about them when a mom and baby whale were spotted not far from us; again we focused on the whales and they appeared! We were all excited spending time with the whales, then off again in search of the dolphins.

I was mentioning how it would be nice if we could all focus on the dolphins when our Kahuna Dolphin, our bottlenose dolphin, appeared at our bow again as it had last year on the 11:11! How was this possible to have a repeat of the same dolphin arriving the same way! This Kahuna dolphin did the same as it had the previous year! Many from the same group Deb had brought the year before were there again, remarking, "The same thing is happening from our 2011 seminar!" We were into oneness once more, again being One.

We all had a fantastic swim with the dolphins. It seemed like a timeless journey. Our goal was to be on the boat at the time of the 12:12 for our meditation and delivery of the whale codes.

At the hour of 12:12, Deb did a heart-inspiring meditation that was so special we all were brought into a bubble of love and light. It opened the way for the Crystalline Whale Codes to be transmitted to the group. As I began to allow the codes to come through me to the others, I could hear some dolphins appear at the bow where we were sitting. The boat was slowly moving through the beautiful waters. I could hear them leaping and jumping with excitement as the codes were being shared. One participant said she couldn't help it and opened her eyes to see two dolphins leap at the same time, making a heart before they entered back into the water.

I could feel messages from the dolphins. They were in ceremony with us, and I was also receiving messages and energies from the whales that we observed nearby on the surface of the water as well as below the water. The whales and dolphins were embracing us with the love, joy, and expansion of all that we are. They combined their bubble of energies with our bubble of energies to become ONE ENERGY FIELD OF LOVE AND LIGHT!

December 21, 2012

Harmony between Masculine and Feminine is like a marriage. Venus is an icosahedron and Mars is a dodecahedron; you put each of these geometries inside the other. Earth is between Venus and Mars. Our existence is to maintain a balance between the masculine and feminine.

The 1999 Solstice put the sun into the darkest part of the solar system. The Dragon Plum Serpent line is the male line. Marcus, an astrology presenter, said: "Whales and Lemuria began in the South Pacific. All the negative, misaligned male energies are to be released, to balance the masculine and feminine on the eclipse. The female and male serpent lines connect at the South Pacific."

The Big Island is at 19.5 degrees latitude on the planetary grid. It resides at one of the points of the Star Tetrahedron, a hyper-dimensional field of energy that can be considered a major stargate portal for the light codes to enter the energetic matrix of the Earth. It has the capacity to broadcast intentions to our world and beyond. This is a time of birthing the Divine Feminine.

December 21, 2012 was said to be the highest frequency to enter Mother Earth at this time. This was the shift of all shifts, the Shift of the Ages, as they were calling it. This was the time of the "Ascension" of the planet and those evolving upon her. I felt the shift, yet some others were upset, saying they hadn't felt or seen the changes that were supposed to occur, as prophesized by the Mayan calendar and other sources.

To me this was an individual shift, happening inside each one of us. Many people expected the shift to happen immediately—like they would wake up the next day and everything would be different, and a new world of peace and harmony would be there for everyone. I never felt that it would happen overnight, but rather that it would be a continual evolving of everyone's energies into more light and consciousness, bringing more peace and harmony to the world. I knew the light would prevail.

We have to go within to create the peace we were looking for within ourselves first, so it can transmit to the world. There were still darker energies to be transformed into light in order for us to be able to move into the Golden Age of love and compassion.

I assisted Joan with her group that week. It was an amazing week of miracles, being with the dolphins who were celebrating with us on our boat trips and all that we were doing at night with our meditations. We gathered on Joan's land to communicate with the ETs by firelight. We had a wonderful time sharing and being together. At the end of our special ceremony I left for Doug and Trish's to present the "Magdalene Codes" to their group. I loved how I moved from group to group in one day!

Activation of the Magdalene Codes

These codes were given to me before I embodied here on Mother Earth. The codes have always been a part of my soul. It wasn't time to transfer these codes until this year. It is only when I am told to do this and when Mary gave her permission to release the codes to others.

Anela played a couple of songs to open our hearts in preparation for the codes to be transferred to each person on this special night. Mary and Jesus created this etheric labyrinth for us to move through while Anela played their angelic music, further raising our vibrations. We continued to ascend as we spiraled up, layer by layer, elevating every cell of our body and attuning us to the frequencies that the 12:12 was anchoring on and into Mother Earth for the Ascension for her Soul, Gaia, as well as our souls.

In the middle of the labyrinth spiral we were met by Mary Magdalene and Jesus, thus reuniting the male and female aspects of ourselves into a unity of Oneness, a Oneness that would propel each of us into a higher frequency of love, light and compassion for all living beings. The codes were then delivered through my Soul Essence from the Soul Essence of Mary Magdalene, and the transference of the Magdalene Codes was complete. Both Mary and Jesus each gave a special blessing for our commitment to being a "Light" for the rest of the world to see and acknowledge within themselves.

We then spiraled back down the labyrinth into our present bodies, grounding all that we had received during the Ascension into our beingness and oneness! Anela started playing festive party music for the celebration and the participants began dancing. My body was in need of quiet after a long day of activations and high energy that was being brought to all of us. I quietly exited, my body filled with overflowing love and joy from all the amazing experiences.

Embodying higher frequencies of Mary Magdalene and Jesus, merging higher frequencies into the cells of my soul, heart, mind and body, I was complete and looking forward to quiet time with my dogs. They always loved feeling these energies, as we shared precious time together.

Animals and humans uniting in love and compassion is the Lemurian Way of Life. It is my way of Life. I thank all the animals that have come into my life to help me learn more about myself, to love unconditionally as the dolphins and whales do. They say dogs, dolphins and whales are all from the same star system, the Sirian system. Feels right to me!

Mt. Shasta–Hawaii Connection

I now live in Hawaii, my spiritual home for the last 17 years, where I have evolved faster since living on this island with our wonderful dolphins, whales, and Pele, our goddess volcano. Both Shasta and the Big Island are Lemuria. They both have volcanoes, near which I have always seemed to live. Both can be very intense at times. They change you at the DNA level, always working to shift us into higher-dimensional frequencies. The Big Island has water and fire, whereas Mt. Shasta has ice and Mountains. I love the balance I receive between the two of them. Both being Lemuria, I have been very blessed by both gifting me with life-altering experiences.

Mt. Shasta Seminar

One wonderful week in July 2011 at Mt. Shasta, Doug and Trish organized a wonderful seminar. Trish had asked me to be the guest speaker and I agreed. Once I began to put material together for my talk, I realized how I was remembering so much more about my past. What a wonderful gift I was receiving as I was reuniting with my past. Hopefully my talk will have others remembering Lemuria, as that is my purpose: to help others experience once more the joy and gifts that are waiting for us in the fifth-dimensional frequencies of Lemuria.

We had a wonderful time exploring sacred sites during the week, enjoying the magical, mystical energies of the Mountain and surrounding area. We had a free night and I felt like going to the Mountain to see if I could have contact with any ET ships. Most of the group decided to go too.

It was a very cold night on the Mountain. We took chairs and after we settled in, I asked if any of my Big Foot friends were nearby. Within a few minutes I felt their Presence. They came slowly, staying behind the trees not far from us. Then I felt many join and begin to surround us, still staying within the trees.

They told me they were the Big Foot group that works closely with the Telosians living within the Mountain. It was as if they were creating a vortex of frequencies as we sat in the middle of this incredible energetic bubble.

We felt we would also have contact with my Sirian Star Ship of One. To my surprise, I began to feel a craft hovering over us, yet it wasn't my Sirian Ship. It was the Ashtar Command, guided by Sananda. I asked if we could come aboard. Their response was yes, if we all came as a group. I asked the group, and they said yes too.

Soon after, I felt lifted up into the ship, as did the others, and each had their own unique experience that was meant for them. When we were back in our chairs, we realized how freezing cold we were. Since time and space isn't the same while visiting the Ashtar Command Ship, we didn't know how long we were there and made ready to go. I have been on their ship many times in Mt. Shasta. They are so loving and beautiful. How could they not be, with Sananda in charge?

The following day, while walking a trail on Shasta with a friend, a man passed by. We smiled and exchanged greetings. Then something in me said, turn around. When we turned only a moment later, he was gone! He still should have been on the trail—where did he go? We both got immediately that this was the Ascended Master St. Germain!

This man, St. Germain, was dressed like a hiker; you would not have thought he would be an Ascended Master! My friend and I had been working in our healing practice with St. Germain for years; we knew that he was at Mt. Shasta assisting many people, overseeing the Mountain. What an amazing gift it was to have him bless us with his Presence.

I have had many mysterious encounters on the Mountain, so for me this was one more magical, mystical experience: an Ascended Master greeting us as a normal-looking person on a trail! These experiences became very normal.

I spent many wonderful times at Mt. Shasta, walking the Mountain in the beautiful springtime with wildflowers in the meadows while enjoying the bliss of being gifted amazing energies and frequencies from the Mountain and the Beings who inhabit and frequent the area: the beloved Telosians and Big Foot.

Metatron: The OM Crystal

Beneath the mega-portal of Mt. Shasta stands an amazing crystal of Atlantis, a crystal of Arcturian origin. It emits the frequency of crystalline platinum and etheric gold. It is used for interdimensional and time travel. It serves as a celestial cosmic port. It will amplify the ability of humans to travel in the astral plane and well beyond. Mt. Shasta is already quite prolific in that capacity. The OM crystal exponentially increases that potential for all who seek such experience there.

It once stood in the great Temple of One on the Atlantean Isle of Poseida. It is referred to as the crystal of Multi-Dimensionality. This sentient crystal is omnipotent in its frequency and holds within its structural alloy of platinum, gold and hyper-quartz the ability to fold, concentrate and amplify that which we think of as light and space. It has 144 facets. The number 144 is a very complex frequency. It represents the code within the golden spiral of all the geometrical base units, termed atoms, in the universe.

The OM crystal was transported through this hyper-dimensional capacity of the inner Earth tunnel system and relocated to Mt. Shasta. The OM Wave of the June 2010 Solstice transmitted hope, love and strength to all who tuned in during the five days of OM, June 19th–23rd. The new Crystalline Network is tuned to the Solstice of OM and will provide further activation of the 144 grids. These crystals are very important to the Crystalline Transition of the grid and planet.

My work with the humpback whales has been to work with the 144,000 crystalline grids of our beloved Mother Earth for the last eight years.

These crystals serve as the blueprint of the new Earth and play a role in creating the Mer-Ka-Ba of humanity. The Law of One is returning, and this time the crystals will not be misused!

2013: Remembrance

This marks the end of this chapter in my life and the end of my writing experience for now. It feels as though my life will be shifting into another timeline of learning more about my Lemurian heritage through life lived in the moment. I am continuing to experience the frequency shifts associated with equinoxes and solstices with a super full moon, so powerful that it seems an accelerated process of evolving has become the norm for many of us living in Kona. All of the Hawaiian Islands are very sacred; being part of Lemuria they are sacred, intense, and amazingly joyful!

I am profoundly blessed as I spend nearly every day with the dolphins and am able to see the humpback whales when they gift us with their presence.

A huge shift took place within my emotional, mental and physical bodies on June 23rd, 2013. During Grandma Chandra's teleconference, we opened a Portal to the Universal Sun of the Suns and rebalanced the Earth's Energy Grids!

At these special times in human history, we are perfectly supported with astrological planetary constellations: Mars-Venus conjunction in the beginning of April, Partial Lunar Eclipse on April 25th, Annular Solar Eclipse on May 10th, the opening of the Portal on May 25th, on June 22nd the Super Full Moon Solstice Portal into the Christos Universal Sun of Suns, and the October Full Moon Lunar Eclipse. Plus more on the way!

We have been preparing ourselves to become an embodiment of Divine Lovers and expanders of higher frequencies of Light to bring the final balance between male and female polarities on Planet Earth.

Eclipses are times of endings and resolution, opportunities to:

Let go of whatever is holding you back in your life
Move to a new level of awareness and insight by accepting
    and ending a cycle of experience
Make peace with the past, present and future
Form honest, open bonds
Be present and honest

The waves of Source energy are moving through the Galactic planes. We are translating light frequency patterns for the living Universe to form the Creation Hologram of the New Living Earth. Our heart is a holographic center. The nature of time is altered; we are entering the time shift. Those who are experiencing divine harmony and joy are the bridge-builders for the New Earth. We are transmitting through the Graille, the living holographic vibration, a bridge of light, and the key to the Isis and Osiris restoration of the living hologram.

Source energies are being transmitted through the Christ Beloved because of the Graille DNA. This is the miracle and the power of the living Graille. Each has their own spiritual calling as part of the living hologram, a Mandala of light we call the 131313. We are the 131313 and we are birthing a world of peace! The Bringers of the Dawn, the Awakeners, each of us tuned into our heart, our inner source of guidance and the source of Universal Oneness that guides the new reality into being here in this plane of existence.

There is nothing now that separates us from Creation. The dark and disturbing veil that covered our planet is lifted, those places no longer exist. Through engaging with these forces, we illuminate the inner realms, permeating the fields of agony and our own sorrows with the Light of Creation and with the Law of Love and universal compassion.

This gives everyone the opportunity to be fully sovereign yet be part of the whole. As souls of light that experience Divine Creation in a new way, a new blueprint for human experience is evolving.

———————————

2013 was a slower year for me, a chance to relax a little more and enjoy sacred time for myself. It has been a good year and I am looking forward to an exciting 2014 (and beyond!) with new experiences for myself, as well as all of you.

MY MANY THANKS AND APRRECIATION TO MY BELOVED GUIDES, TEACHERS OF LIGHT, ANGELS AND FAIRIES, DOLPHINS AND WHALES, AND MY SPECIAL COMPANIONS, MY DOGS NOEL AND MAGDALENE (MADDIE), WHO BLESSED MY HOME THE DAY MY SHEBA WAS LAID TO REST. TO THE LOVING MEMORY OF MY LITTLE MASTER DOG, BABAJI, NICKEA, AMBER AND SWEET SHEBA, I LOVE YOU AND MISS YOUR PHYSICAL PRESENCE. I KNOW YOU ARE ALWAYS WITH ME FOR THERE IS NO SEPARATION: THERE IS ONLY LOVE!

I hope you enjoyed my journey as I was learning and experiencing some of the most amazing and inspiring times in my life from three years old to the present. I have had many healings and learned so much about myself through this journey into the unknown world and the known world most of us are living in at this time.

My purpose for writing this book was to be of assistance to others who may have had similar experiences, yet possibly weren't sure if they were real. Or perhaps felt it wasn't something they could share, afraid of what others might think or say. If you had similar encounters and felt that you might be looked at as crazy, then I would say to you: you know what your experience was better than anyone else. See your experiences as a blessing, for that is what they are. Unusual, yes; real, yes—and in those moments your life was being changed on some level forever.

Not everyone would believe some of what I have experienced; yet if we were changed for the better, then isn't that the most important thing to us? It is our truth and no one can take that away from us, whether they believe in Fairies, Angels, UFOs, Big Foot, ETs, or beings that are unseen to most people. It doesn't mean they are not real.

If healing was brought to you, in even a small way, that was the reason the Fairies, Angels, Dolphins, Whales, Big Foot and ETs wanted me to share this story with you, so you could receive healing and inspiration. This is what they are all about, as am I. I couldn't have written this chapter in my life without their assistance.

Most of my life I have been receiving their guidance, especially when I was tuned in and aware. They have shared messages with me so I could experience the highest light for myself and others. I can't leave out the Source of All That Is, Divine Love and Truth, my Masters and Teachers of Light, my Higher Essence Self, and the Lemurian Dreamers who helped me to Dream my Dream into existence.

How could I ever feel alone in this world when I have so much Help? Sometimes I have to remember to ask for assistance when I require it, as I am still learning every day to be more aware of my environment. This I have learned from the dolphins and whales.

May you be blessed beyond what you can imagine, beyond your beliefs and concepts, as you enter the fifth-dimensional consciousness into paradise, into Lemuria!

I'm looking forward to seeing you all there. What fun we will all have playing in love, peace, harmony and joy!

Biography

Celeste brings forth inspiration and teachings from the Angelic and Fairy Realms, the Ascended Masters, Beings of Light and Love, ET Beings, Whales and Dolphins, Star Beings, and those of her spiritual lineage/heritage: the Lemurians.

Celeste is a Healer of the Soul, Heart, Mind, and Body who brings each person into their perfected Balance and Radiance. Through her Soul embodiment of Ke Waine Ka Kalima, she acts as the "Protectress of the Oceans and Seas and all that live within these waters." She facilitates swimming with dolphins in Kona, Hawaii, and with humpback whales in the Kingdom of Tonga. Her Essence resides in All Nature with the Nature Spirits.

She was born in Fort Bragg on the California coast and lived with her family in Point Arena. At age three, angels taught her how to communicate and speak with them through her dolls, without anyone knowing she was talking with angels. She continues to speak with Angelic friends today, as she herself is of the Angelic Realm.

She moved to Red Bluff, California at age nine. Both these areas are considered Big Foot country and she was a child of nature. Her first physical encounter was at her home at the age of 18. Later, while living in Oregon, she had many physical and nonphysical contacts with her sixth-dimensional group of Big Foot that has been guiding her.

Being of Lemurian heritage and living in the remaining areas of Lemuria her whole life, she now calls Kona, Hawaii home. Here, for the last 17 years she has enjoyed near-daily dolphin swims and lives in Lemurian Paradise. She facilitates groups to swim with dolphins and leads groups to Tonga to swim with South Pacific humpback whales.

In Gratitude

I am grateful to the following people, who have been a source of Love, Inspiration and Joy in my life: my daughters Reneé and Kimberlee; my grandchildren, Jessica, Morgan, Caton and Jack Henry; my great-grandson Kameron Henry. Thank you all for being in my life, teaching me as much as I hopefully have taught you. To my late husband Henry, you gave me so much: 33 years of learning and trusting in myself, helping me to be more of who I am. You will live in my memory forever. My wonderful family, you are deeply loved and appreciated.

My sincere thanks and gratitude go to my wonderful editor, Dana Tomasino, for her tireless hours and devotion to fine-tuning this personal account of my story. Her work has made my book more presentable for my readers, so they can live my life adventures with me as they read and experience the spaces between the words, which is where the Essence of Spirit lives.

To my many wonderful, amazing friends: A special thanks to Trish Regan, my special angel, for reading my book, helping to make it flow, and giving me inspiration. To Michael Sean for initial editing and organization of my book. To mention a few of my close angel friends who have inspired my life with your friendship: Doug Hackett, Joan, Connie, Belinda, Ru, Kathy, Sheila, Michael, Anita and Rika, my extended family, Susan, Analiah, Dean, Candy, Aurora, Carina and Stephanie, Bernie, Alorah, Debra, Heartmoon, Douglas, Gina, Lisa, Sheoli, Jan, Al, Thomas, Ed and Kathy, and so many others. All of my Tonga whale friends, my community dolphin podners whom I swim with: I love and appreciate you so much. There are many more to name, and you know who you are. Thank you all so much for your friendship and love. You are all very special to me. I will never forget your Presence.

Artwork by Eva M. Sakmar-Sullivan